Atlas symbols

C000184886

Scale 1:190,000 or 3 miles to 1 inch (1.9km to 1cm) Some islands are shown at smaller scales and northern Scotland at 1:250,000 scale.

Motoring information

M4	Motorway with number	
Toll	Toll motorway with toll station	
11	Motorway junction with and without number	
3	Restricted motorway junctions	
S Fleet	Motorway service area	
	Motorway and junction under construction	
A3	Primary route single/dual carriageway	
	Primary route junction with and without number	
3	Restricted primary route junctions	
S	Primary route service area	
BATH	Primary route destination	
A1123	Other A road single/dual carriageway	
B2070	B road single/dual carriageway	
	Minor road more than 4 metres wide, less than 4 metres wide	
	Roundabout	
	Interchange/junction	

	Narrow primary/other A/B road with passing places (Scotland)	
	Road under construction	
	Road tunnel	
Toll	Road toll, steep gradient (arrows point downhill)	
5	Distance in miles between symbols	
P·R	Park and Ride location (at least 6 days per week)	
or V	Vehicle ferry	
	Fast vehicle ferry or catamaran	

	Railway line, in tunnel	
	Railway station and level crossing	
	Tourist railway	
	City, town, village or other built-up area	
H F	Airport, heliport, international freight terminal	
H	24-hour Accident & Emergency hospital	
C	Crematorium	
	Sandy beach	

30	Safety camera site (fixed location) with speed limit in mph	
40	Section of road with two or more fixed safety cameras, with speed limit in mph	
50 50	Average speed (SPECS™) camera system with speed limit in mph	
V	Fixed safety camera site with variable speed limit	
628 ▲	Height in metres	
637 Lecht Summit	Mountain pass	
	National boundary	
	County, administrative boundary	

Touring information To avoid disappointment, check opening times before visiting.

Scenic route	Museum or art gallery	Aquarium	Steam railway centre	National Trust for Scotland property
Tourist Information Centre	Industrial interest	National Nature Reserve (England, Scotland, Wales)	Cave	English Heritage site
Tourist Information Centre (seasonal)	Aqueduct or viaduct	Local nature reserve	Windmill, monument	Historic Scotland site
Visitor or heritage centre	Garden	Wildlife Trust reserve	Golf course (AA listed)	Cadw (Welsh heritage) site
Picnic site	Arboretum	RSPB site	County cricket ground	Other place of interest
Caravan site (AA inspected)	Vineyard	Forest drive	Rugby Union national stadium	Boxed symbols indicate attractions within urban areas
Camping site (AA inspected)	Country park	National trail	International athletics stadium	World Heritage Site (UNESCO)
Caravan & camping site (AA inspected)	Agricultural showground	Viewpoint	Horse racing, show jumping	National Park
Abbey, cathedral or priory	Theme park	Hill-fort	Motor-racing circuit	National Scenic Area (Scotland)
Ruined abbey, cathedral or priory	Farm or animal centre	Roman antiquity	Air show venue	Forest Park
Castle	Zoological or wildlife collection	Prehistoric monument	Ski slope (natural, artificial)	Heritage coast
Historic house or building	Bird collection	Battle site with year 1066	National Trust property	Major shopping centre

12th edition June 2014

© AA Media Limited 2014

Original edition printed 2003

Cartography:
All cartography in this atlas edited, designed and produced by the Mapping Services Department of AA Publishing (A05189).

This product contains Ordnance Survey data © Crown copyright and database right 2014 and Royal Mail data © Royal Mail copyright and database right 2014.

Land & Property Services Paper Map Licensed Partner This is based upon Crown Copyright and is reproduced with the permission of Land & Property Services under delegated authority from the Controller of Her Majesty's Stationery Office, © Crown copyright and database right 2014. PMLPA No. 100497.

Ordnance Survey Ireland's National Mapping Agency © Ordnance Survey Ireland/Government of Ireland Copyright Permit No. MP0000314.

Acknowledgements:
AA Publishing would like to thank the following for their assistance in producing this atlas:
RoadPilot® Information on fixed speed camera locations provided by and © 2014 RoadPilot® Driving Technology.
Crematoria data provided by the Cremation Society of Great Britain. Cadw, English Heritage, Forestry Commission, Historic Scotland, Johnsons, National Trust and National Trust for Scotland, RSPB, The Wildlife Trust, Scottish Natural Heritage, Natural England, The Countryside Council for Wales (road maps).

Printer:
Printed in Britain by Wyndeham Peterborough Ltd.

Route planner

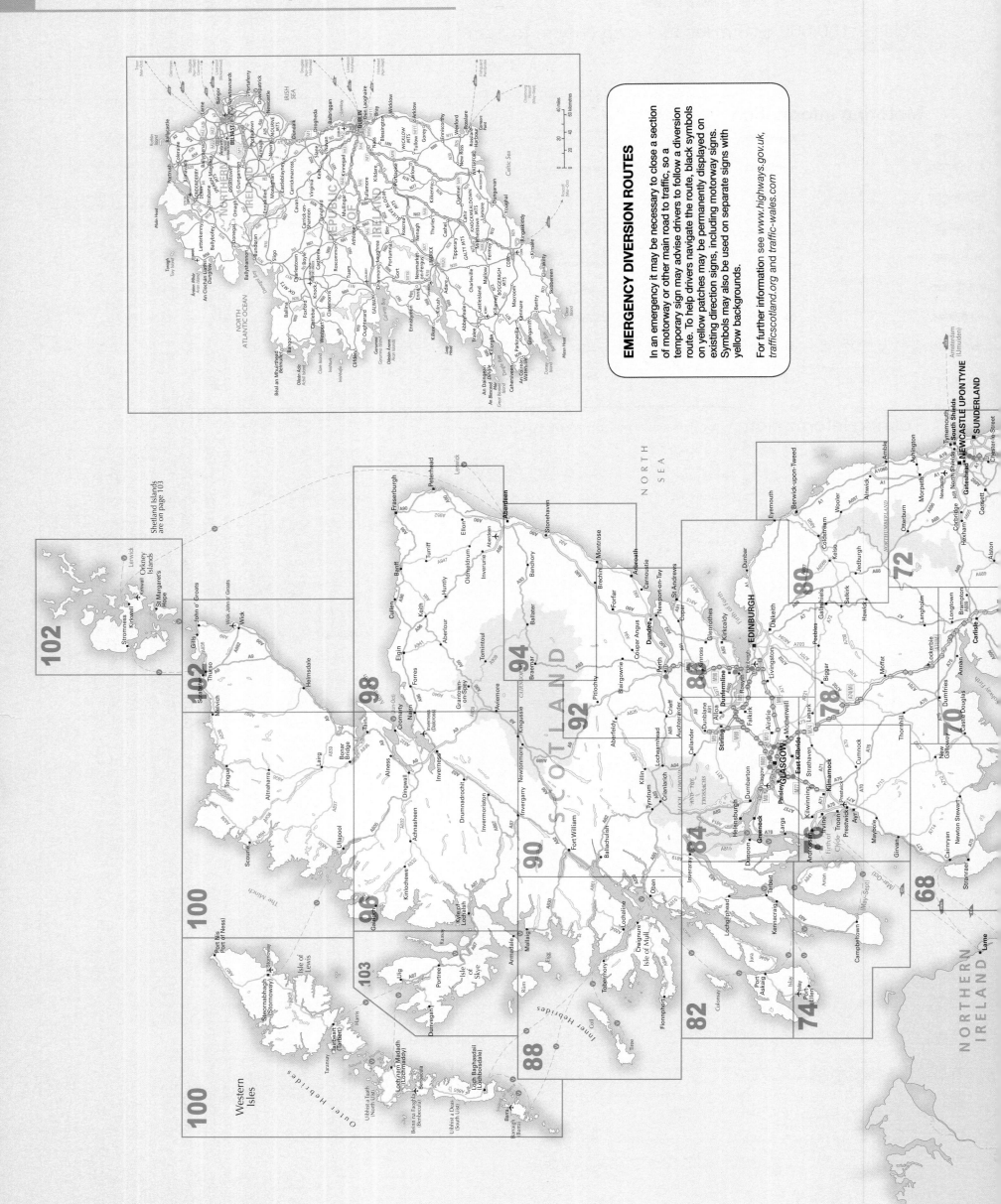

Shetland Islands are on page 103

EMERGENCY DIVERSION ROUTES

In an emergency it may be necessary to close a section of motorway or other main road to traffic, so a temporary sign may advise drivers to follow a diversion route. To help drivers navigate the route, black symbols on yellow patches may be permanently displayed on existing direction signs, including motorway signs. Symbols may also be used on separate signs with yellow backgrounds.

For further information see www.highways.gov.uk, trafficscotland.org and traffic-wales.com

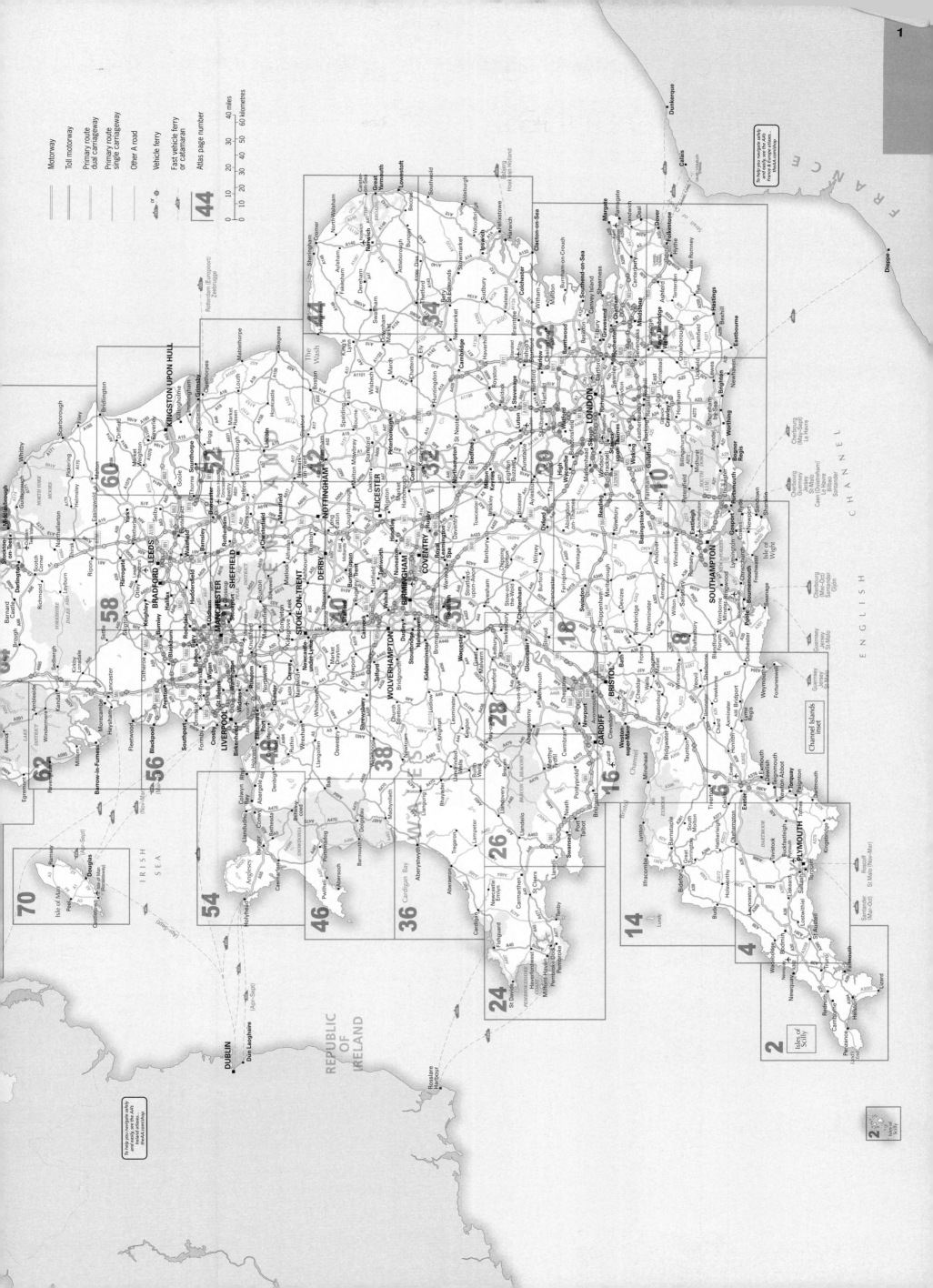

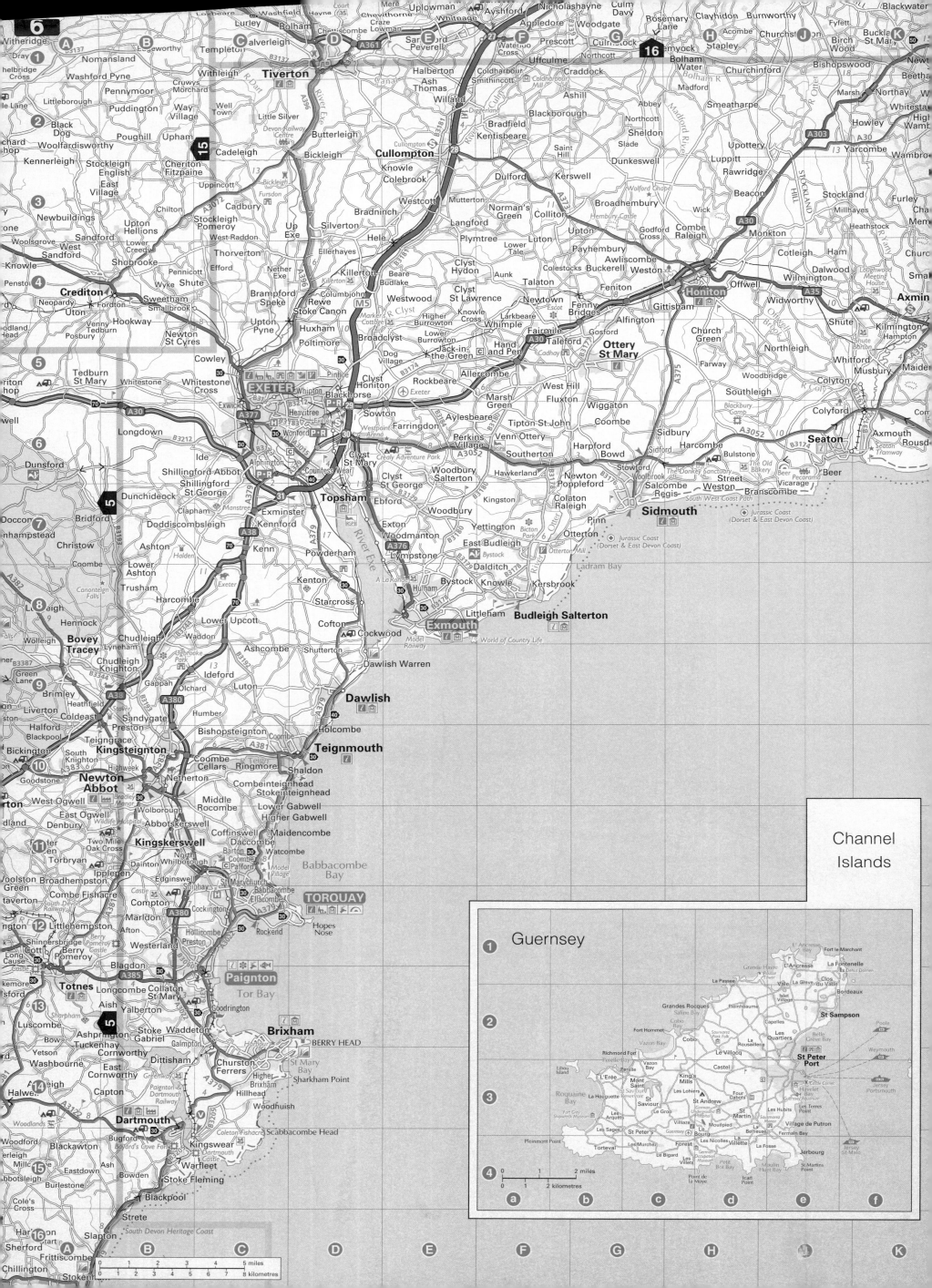

North West
Point

*Lundy
Heritage Coast*

LUNDY

▲142

Marisco

Shutter Point   Surf Point

B A R N S T A P L E

O R

B I D E F O R D   B A Y

Bull
Point
Rockham
Bay
Morte
Mortehoe
Point
Woolacombe
Morte
Bay
Baggy   Pickwell
Point   Putsborough
Croyde Bay   Georgeham
Croyde Bay   Croyde   Darrac
B3231
Saunton
Braunton
Braunton
Burrows
North Devon
Heritage Coast
Crow
Point
Northam
Burrows
Appledore
Westward Ho!   Northam
B3236
Eastleig
East-the-W

HARTLAND POINT   Shipload
Bay
Titchberry   Brownsham
Damehole
Point   Hartland Abbey
& Gardens
Stoke   Velly   Clovelly
Hartland Quay   B3248   Higher   Buck's
Clovelly   Mills
Spekes Mill   Hartland   Horns
Mouth   Docton Mill   Woodtown   Cross
Milford   Gardens   Milky Way   Buck's   A39
Edistone   Philham   Cross   Goldworthy
Elmscott   Tosberry   Woolfardisworthy   Parkham
Hardisworthy   Cranford   Parkham
South   Ash
Hole   Melbury
Welcombe   Ashmansworthy
Mead   East
Darracott   Meddon   Putford   Thornehillhead
Gooseham   Woolley   West
Mill   Eastcott   16   East   Dinworthy   Putford
Gooseham   Youlstone   Gnome   Colscott   Haytown
Morwenstow   Reserve ★
Higher Sharpnose Point   West Youlstone   Bradworthy   Bulkworthy
South West   Shop   A39   Kimworthy   Abbots
Coast Path   Woodford   Tamar   Bickington   Newton
Lower Sharpnose Point   Lakes   Sutcombe   Venngreen   St Petrock
Steeple Point   Kilkhampton   Alfardisworthy   Milton
Stibb   Sutcombemill   River   Damerel
Sandy   Thurdon   Soldon   Thornbury   Shebbear
Mouth   Dunsden   Soldon   Woodacott   Bradford
Northcott   Maer   Cross   Holsworthy   Brendon   Lashbrook
Mouth   Poughill   Bush   Hersham   Beacon   Cookbury   Holemoor
Bude Castle   Flexbury   Grimscott   Lana   Chilsworthy   Cookbury
Bude   Stratton   Launcells   Kingford   Anvil   Wick
Bay   Launcells   Cross   Pancrasweek   Corner   A3072
Lynstone   Red Post   A3072   Derril   Derriton   Holsworthy   Hollacombe   Brandis
Upton   Buttsbear   Pyworthy   Corner
Helebridge   Cross   Whimble   Headon   Chilla
Marhamchurch   Bridgerule   Chasty
Widemouth   Titson   Leworthy   Buckhorn   Halwill
Bay   Box's Shop   Junction
Millook   Coppathorne   Kitleigh   Clawton   Langaford   Beaworthy
Dizzard Point   Bangors   Whitstone   East   Quoditch   Stowford
Dizzard   Poundstock   Balsdon   Higher
Penlean   Treskinnick   North Tamerton   Nethercott   Prestacott
St   Tregole   Cross   Week   Lana   Ashwater   Ashmill
Gennys   Coxford   St Mary   Luffincott   West   Henford
Crackington Haven   Rosecare   Jacobstow   Peeke   Bradaford   Eworthy
Cambeak   Wainhouse   Southcott   Maxworthy   West Curry   Chapmans   Virginstow   Germansweek
Sweets   Corner   B3263   Trengune   South Wheatley   Clubworthy   Well
Beeny   A39   Marshgate   Canworthy   Troswell   Northcott   East Panson   Grinacombe
Witchcroft   Water   Copthorne   Boyton   West   Moor
Tresparrett   Lesnewth   Eter   Billacott   Brazacott   South   Panson   Sitcott   Broadwoodwidger
Boscastle   Treworld   Trelash   Warbstow   Trillacott   Beer   Langdon   Downicary
Otterham   North Petherwin   Bridgetown   St Giles-on-

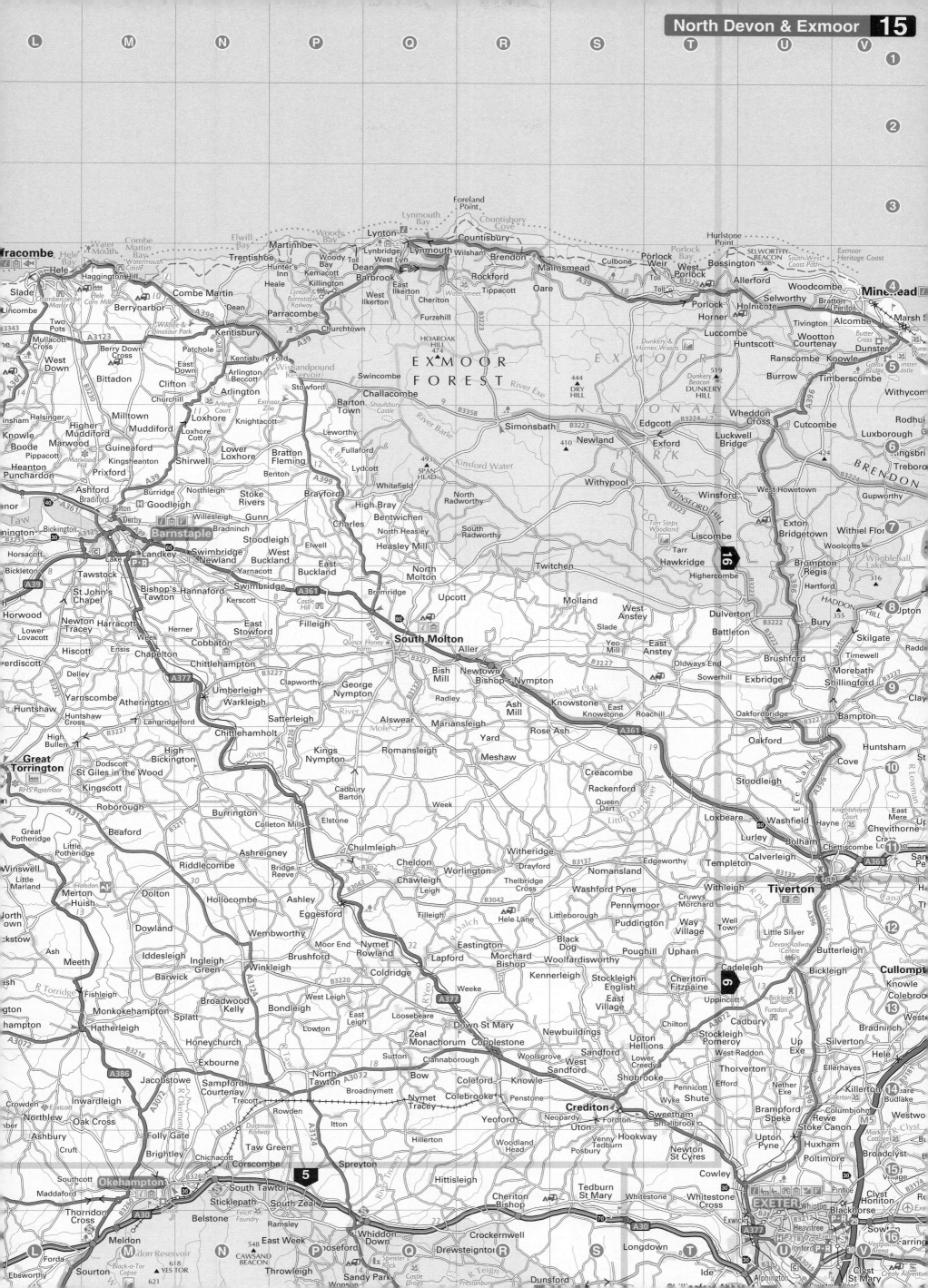

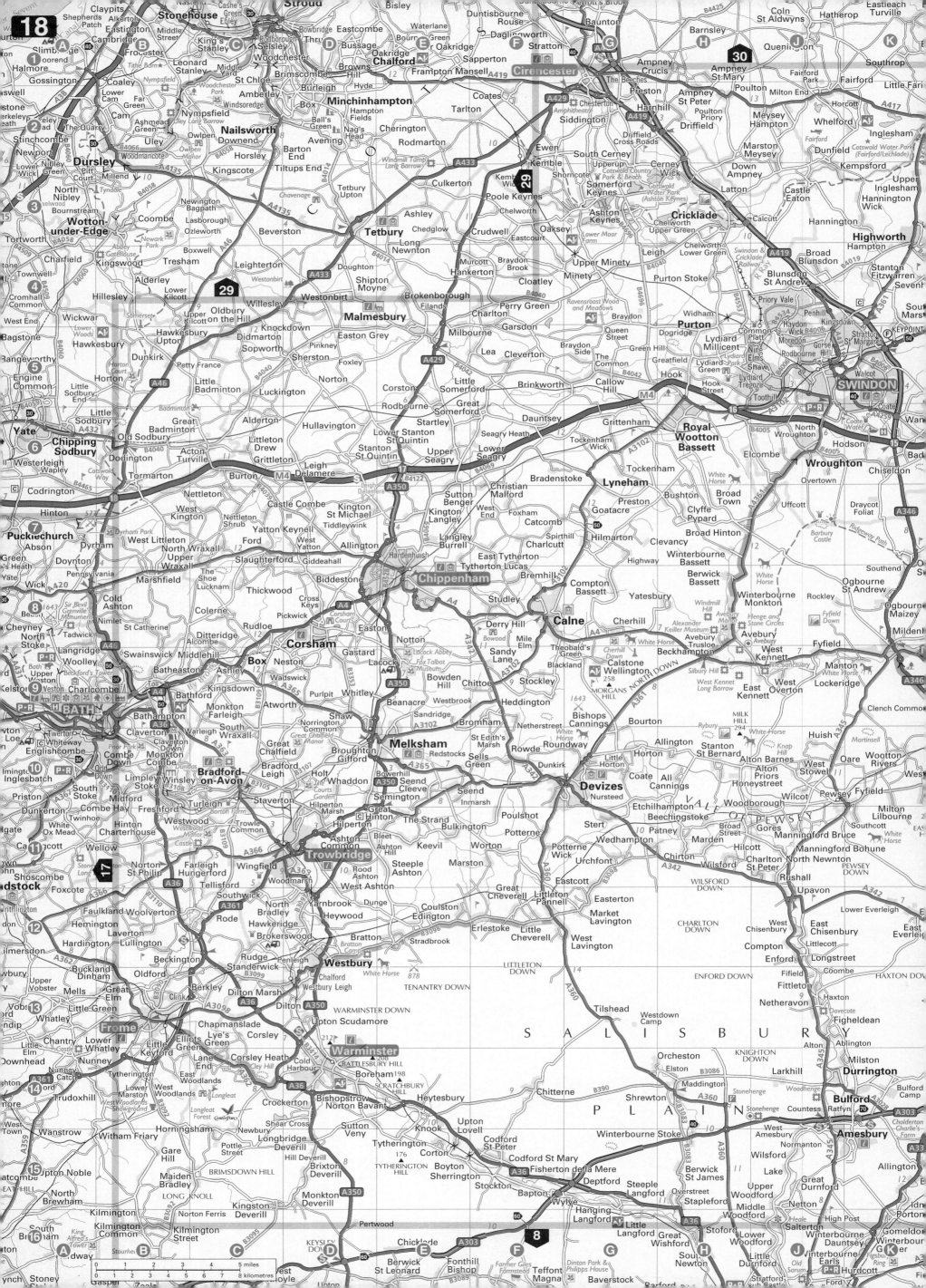

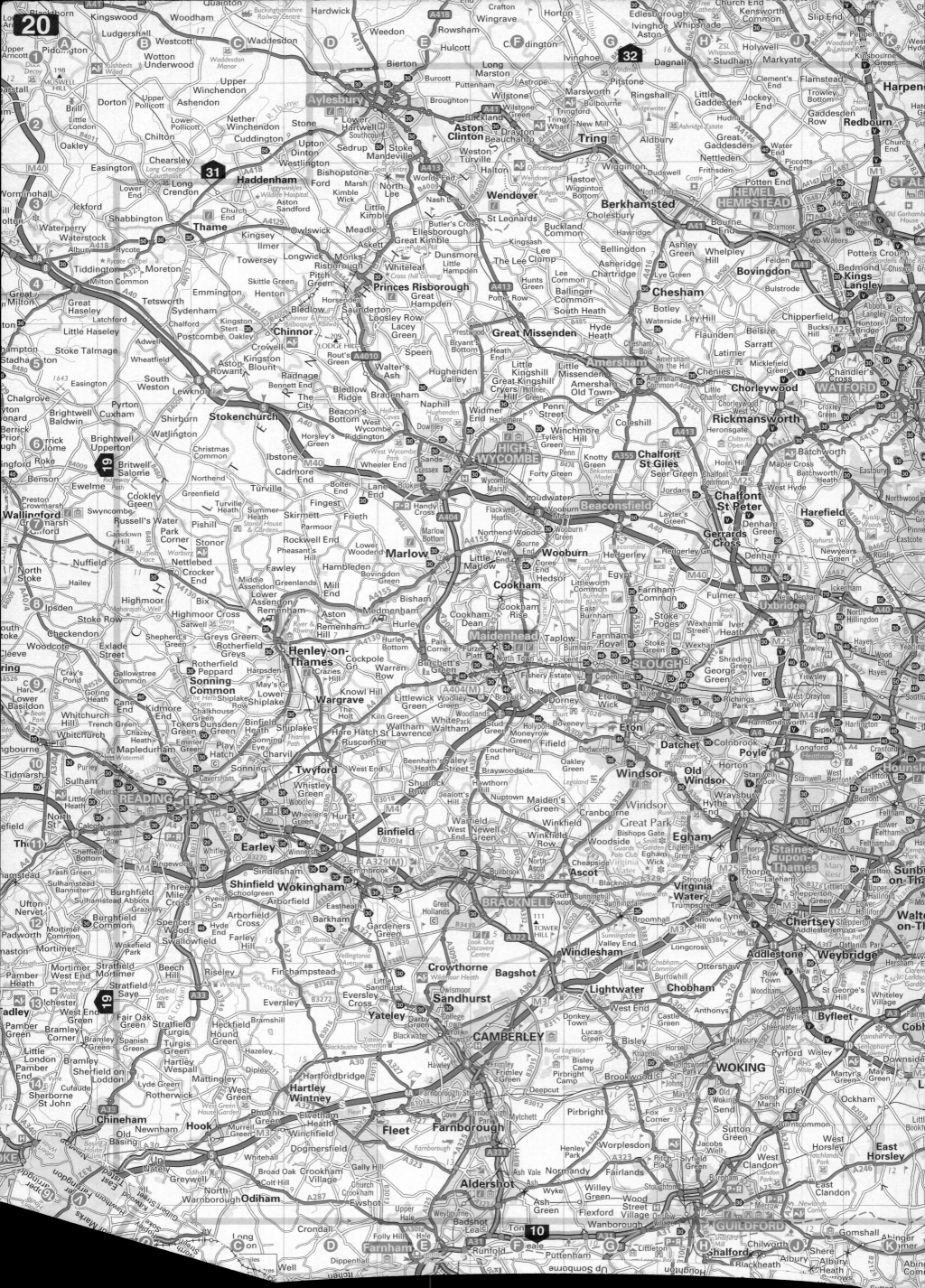

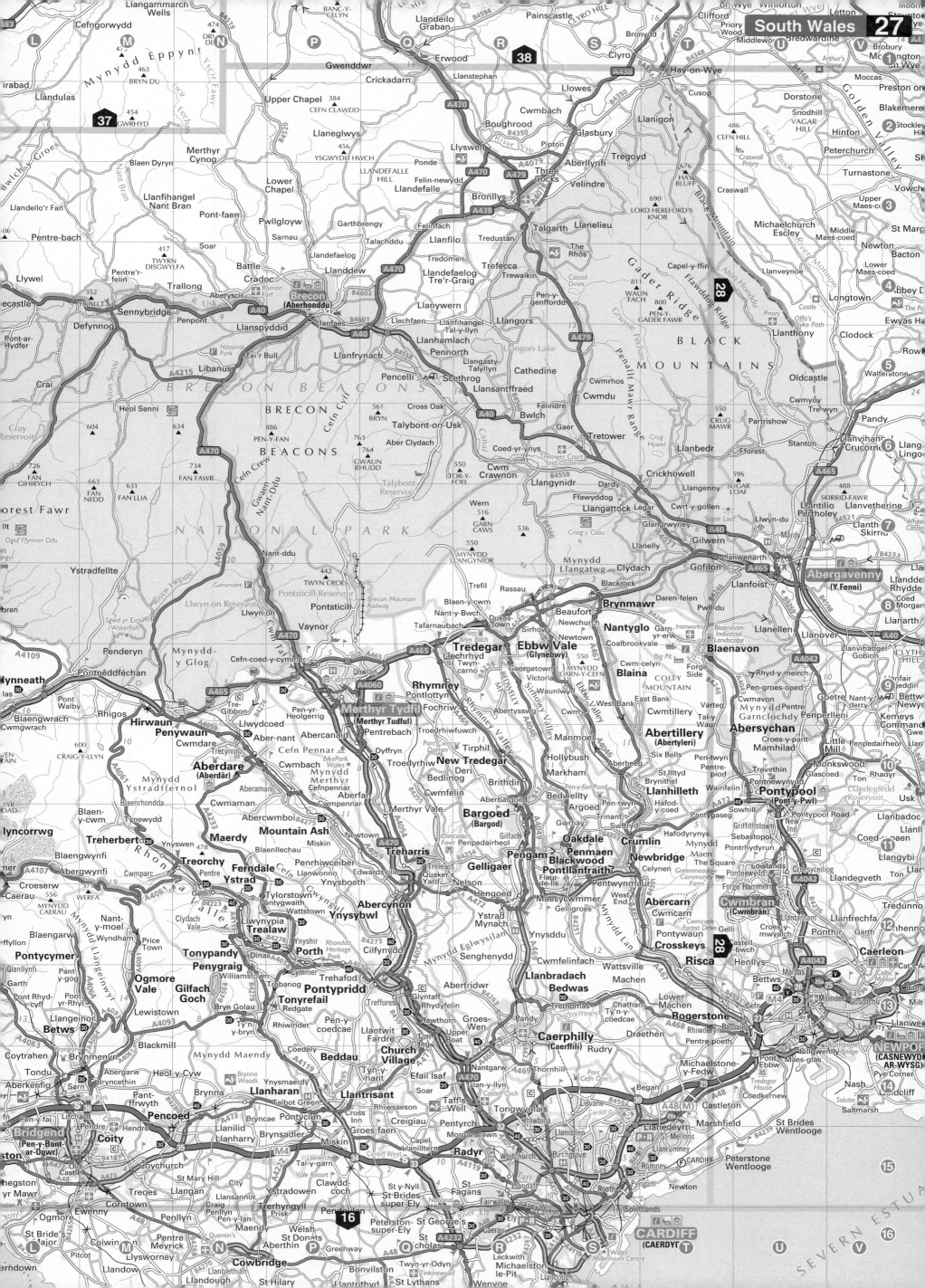

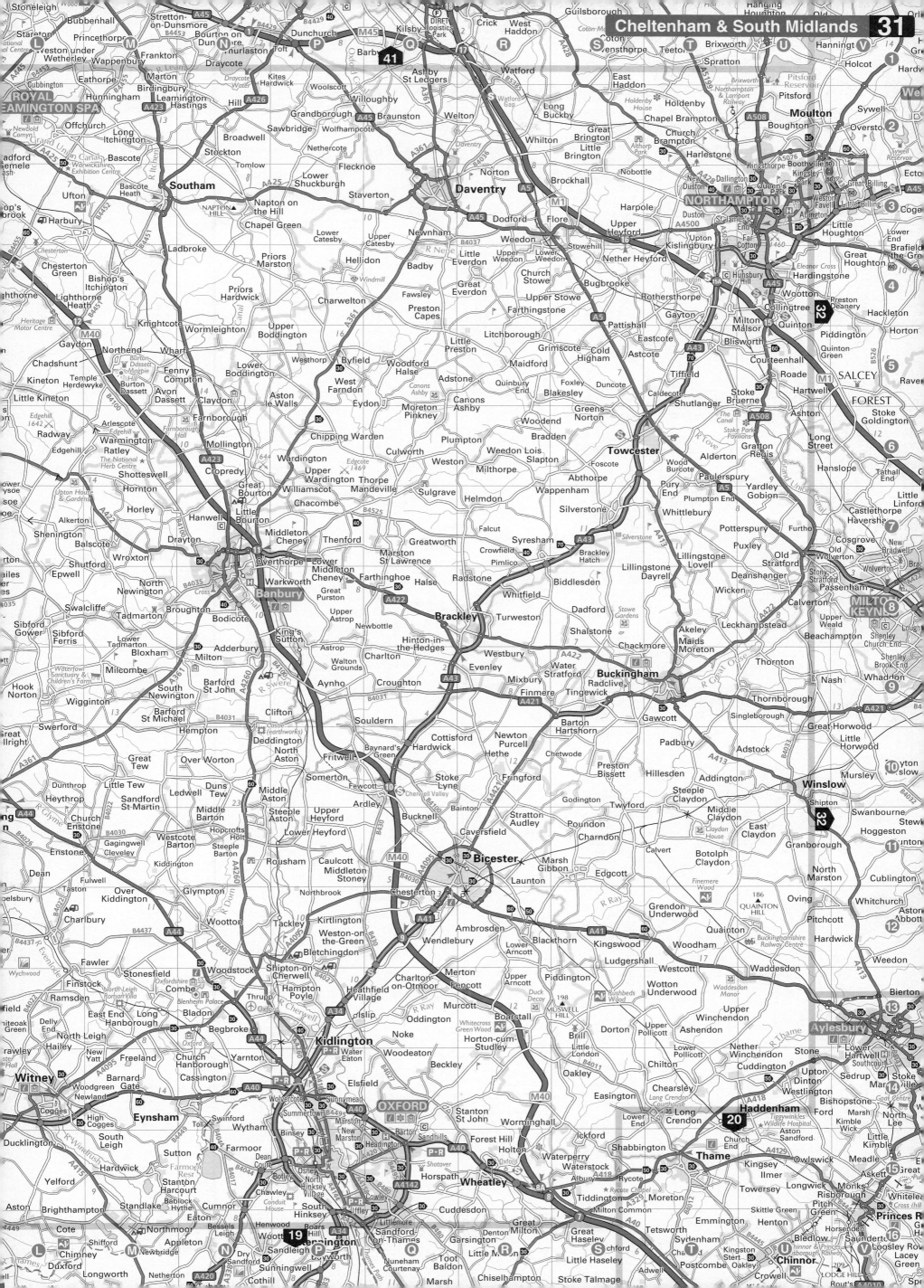

C A R D I G A N

B A Y

Llanrh
Llansantffraid
Llanon
Aberarth
Aberaeron
Pennant
Monac
New Quay
Llyswen
Foss-y-ffin
Llanina
Llwyncelyn
A482
Maen-y-groes
Gilfachrheda
Newb
Cross
Inn
Llanarth
Oakford
Ceredigion Heritage Coast
Cwmtydu
Nanternis
Caerwedros
Ciliau
Aeron
Ynys-Lochtyn
Llwyndafydd
Pentre'rbryn
Dihewyd
Mydroilyn
Ystrad
Aeron
Llangrannog
Pontgarreg
Synod Inn
Tempi
Morfa
Plwmp
Ffynnonddewi
Cae Hir
Penbryn
Pentregat
311
Aberporth
Sarnau
Pentregat
Talgarreg
Gorsgoch
Cardigan
Island
Ceredigion
Heritage Coast
Mwnt
Parcllyn
Tresaith
Brynhoffnant
324
Bwlchyfadfa
Felinwynt-Rainforest
& Butterfly Centre
Cardigan Island
Coastal Farm Park
Y Ferwig
Blaenannerch
Tan-y-groes
Glynarthen
Rhydlewis
Capel
Cynon
Cwrt-newydd
Gwbert on Sea
Tremain
A487
Blaenporth
Ffostrasol
Pontshaen
Cwmsychbant
Llanwn
Poppit
Sands
Penparc
Bettws
Evan
Hawen
Penrhiw-pal
Tre-groes
Drefach
Pembrokeshire
Coast Path
Abbey &
Coach House
Cardigan
(Aberteifi)
Beulah
Troedyraur
Maesllyn
Prengwyn
Llanwenog
St Dogmaels Moylgrove
Heritage Coast
St-Dogmaels
Llangoedmor
B4570
Ponthirwaun
Brongest
Coed-
y-Bryn
Croes-lan
Rhydowen
Llanybydder
Geibwr Bay
Bridgend
Llechryd
Llandygwydd
Langynllo
A475
Moylgrove
Monington
Glanrhyd
Pen-y-
bryn
Teifi
Marshes
A484
Cilgerran
NVY SIDE
Cwm-
cou
Aber-
banc
Gorrig
258
Capel
Dewi
rwyn-y-bwa
A487
Bridell
Abercych
Cenarth
Adpar
Llandyfriog
Penrhiw-llan
Horeb
Rock Mill
Woollen &
Water Mill
Rhuddlan
Newport
Bay
Tredrissi
B4582
Pontgarreg
Pen-rhiw
Teifi Valley
Railway
Llandysul
Llanfihangel-
ar-arth
Llanfi-giar-
Bryn-
Hellan
Berry Hill
Nevern
A478
Rhoshill
Newcastle
Emlyn
(Castell Newydd Emlyn)
Aber-
arad
Pentre-
cagel
Hanllwni
Dir
Parrog
Newport
Felindre
Farchog
Pengelli
Forest
Newchapel
Henllan
Pontwelly
B4336
Mynydd
Llanllwni
Pontf
Castell
Carreg
Coetan
19
Eglwyswrw
B4332
Boncath
25
nrherber
Drefach
Felindre
National
Wool
Saron
Pentre-cwrt
26
Crosswell
Pontygynon
Llanfair
Nant-Gwyn
Whitechurch
Blaenffos
Capel Iwan
Cwmhiraeth
Glynteg
Drefelin
Banc-y-
ffordd
Pencader
New Inn
369
Brynberian
Pontyglasier
21
Bwlch-y-groes
Clydey
335
Cwmpengraig
257
23
Gwyddgrug
PEMBROKESHIRE COAST
Crymych
Star
Cilrhedyn
Cwm
Morgan
362
Rhos
Dol-gran
358
Gwer
NATIONAL PARK
Hermon
Tegryn
Llwyn-
drain
B4299
Cwmduad
Alltwalis

0   1   2   3   4   5 miles
0   1   2   3   4   5   6   7   8 kilometres

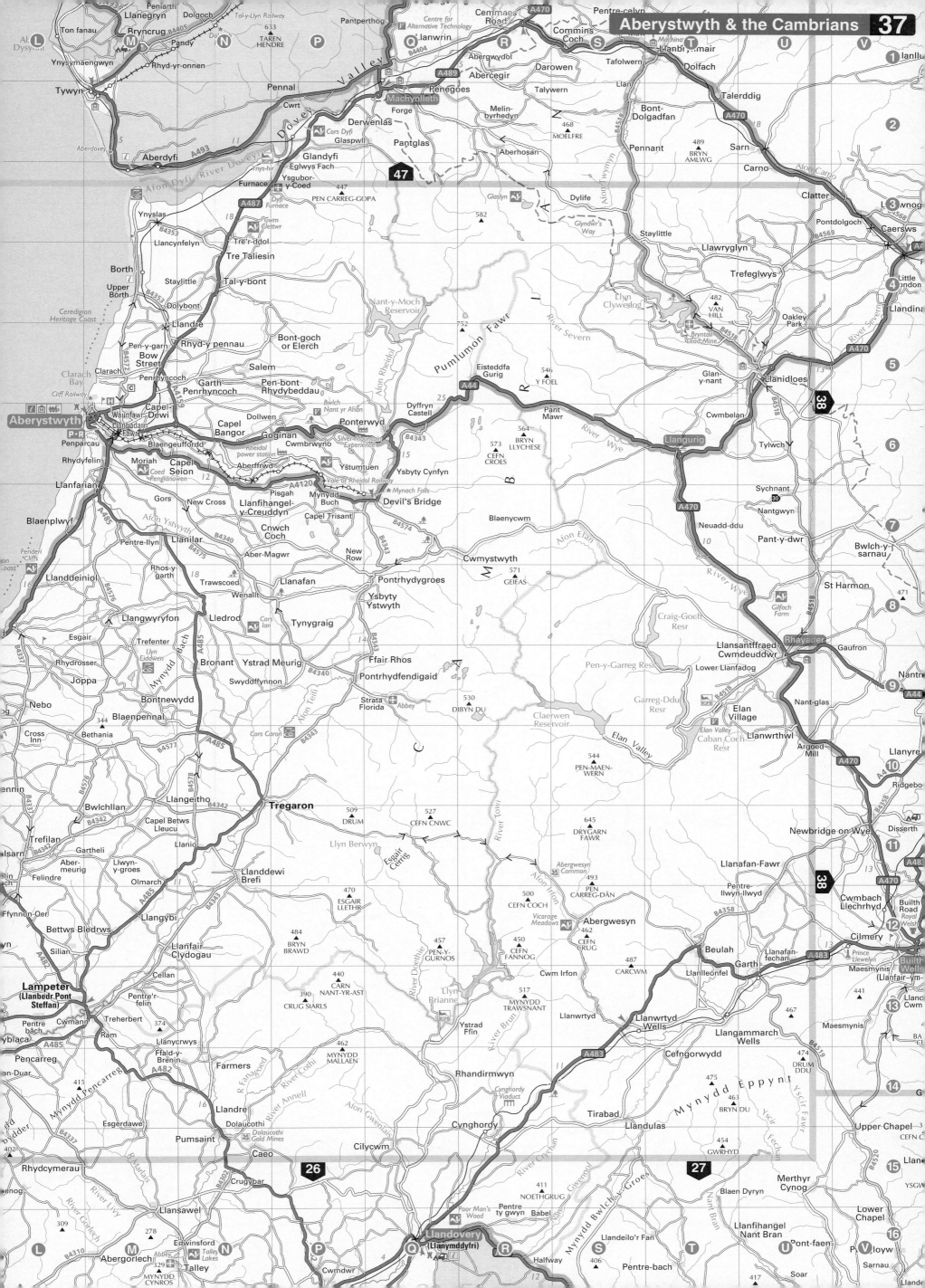

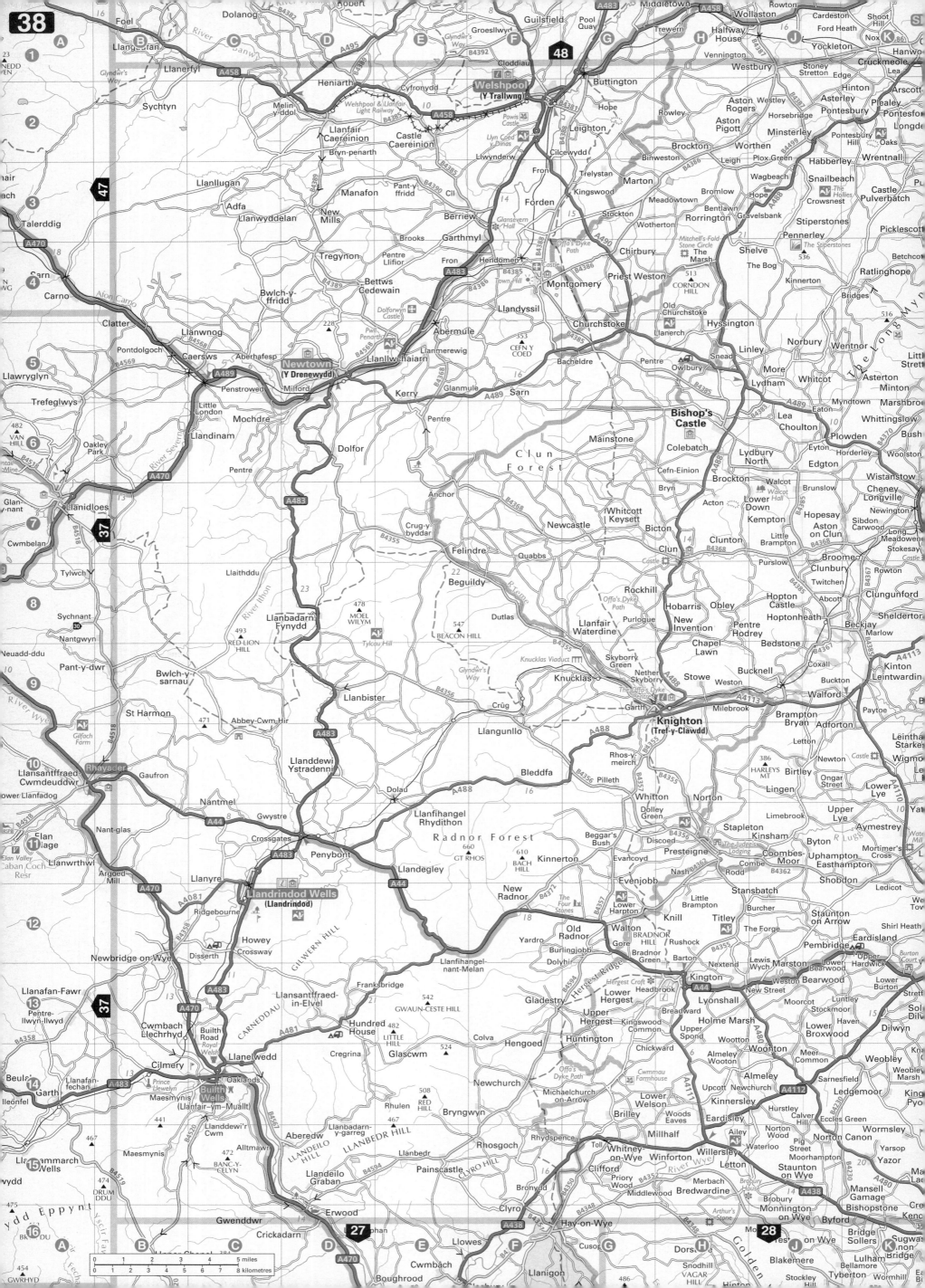

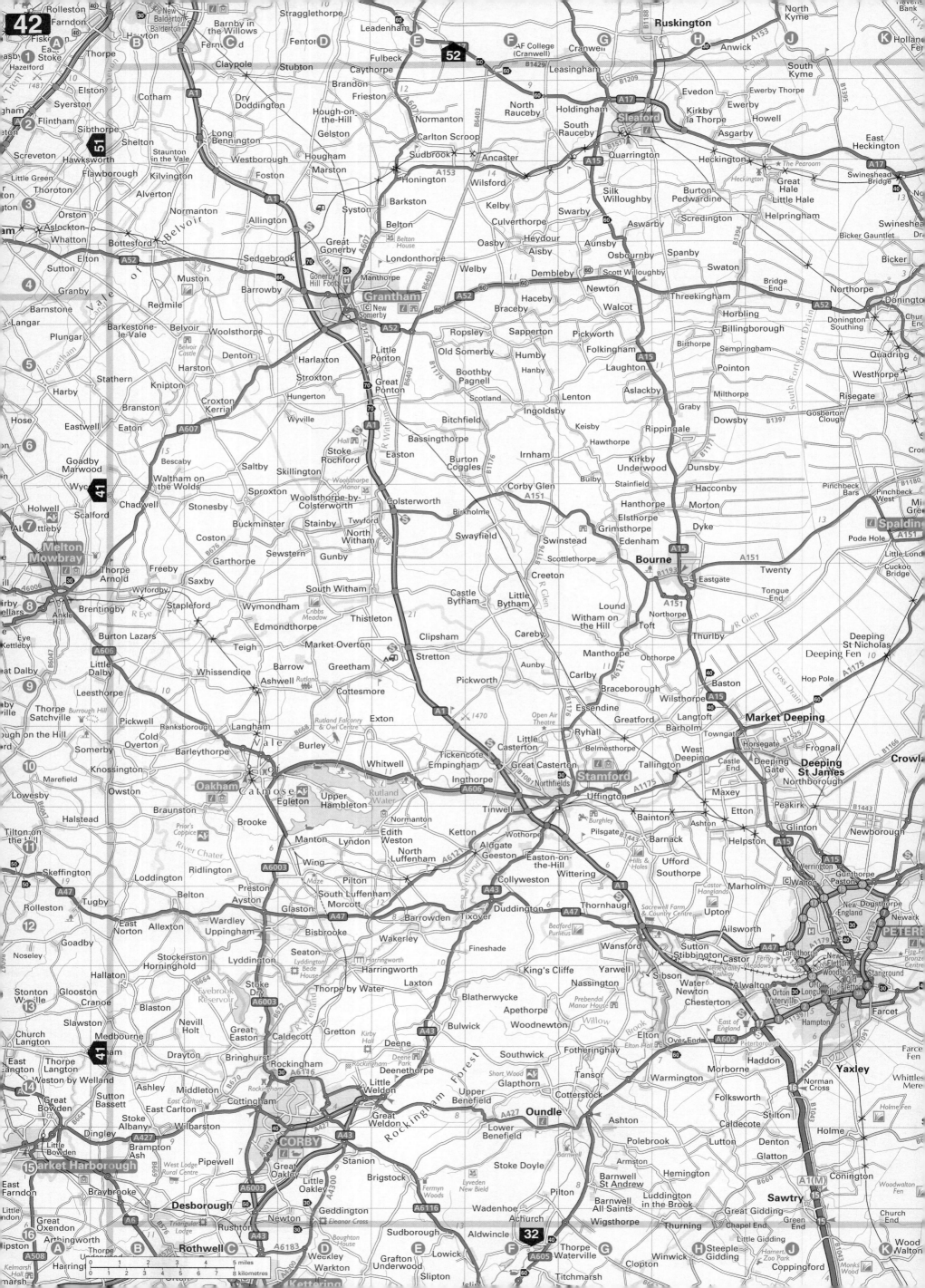

A B C D E F G H

1

CAERNARFON

2

BAY

3

54

4

5

6

7

8

9

10

11

12

13

CARDIGAN

14

BAY

15

16

A B C D E F G H J K

Morfa Dinlle
Llanwnda
Rhostryfan
Rhosgadfan
Penyffridd
Moel
Dinas Dinlle
Llandwrog
Groeslon
Carmel
Cilgwyn
Fron
Nant
Penygroes
Talysarn
Slateworks
Aberdesach
Pontllyfni
Llanllyfni
Tai'n Lôn
Nebo
Clynnog-fawr
Capeluchaf   19
Nasareth
Gyrn-goch
Pant Glas
Lleyn Heritage Coast
Trefor
Y GYRN-DDU   522
PENINSULA
Bryncir
Garn-Dolbenmaen
Dolbe
Tre'r Ceiri
564   Llanaelhaearn
Glan-Dwyfach
Trwyn y Grolech
YR EIFL   20
21
St Cybi's Well
Rhoslan
Llithfaen
Llwyndyrys
Pencaenewydd
Llangybi
Pistyll
Fron   B4354
Y Ffor
Llanarmon
Llanystumdwy
Pentrefeli
Carreg Ddu
Porth Nefyn
Nefyn
Rhos-fawr
B4354
Chwilog   13
Criccieth
Morfa Nefyn
Edern
Bodfuan
Llannor
Abererch
Penarth Fawr Medieval House
Castle
Porth Dinllaen
Groesffordd
Efailnewydd
Porth Ysgaden
Rhos-y-llan
Tudweiliog
Dinas
LLEYN
B4415
Llanbedrog
Denio
Pen-ychain
Rhyd-y-clafdy
Porth Colman
Carn Fadrun   371
Pwllheli
Tremad
Pen-y-graig
Brynmawr   14
Llaniestyn
Garnfadryn
Penrhos   7
Llangwnnadl
Meyllteyrn
Mynytho
Trwyn Llanbedrog
Sarn
Botwnnog
Nanhoron
St Tudwal's Road
Bryncroes
Llandegwning
Rhydlios
Rhoshirwaun
Porthor
Llangian
Abersoch
Penycaerau
Plas yn Rhiw
Y Rhiw
Llanengan
Sarn Bach
St Tudwal's Island East
Anelog
Bwlchtocyn
Marchros
Porth Neigwl or Hell's Mouth
St Tudwal's Island West
Uwchmynydd
Aberdaron
Llanfaelrhys
Porth Ysgo
Aberdaron Bay
Porth Geiriad
Lleyn Heritage Coast
Bardsey Sound
St Mary's
Ynys Enlli
BARDSEY ISLAND

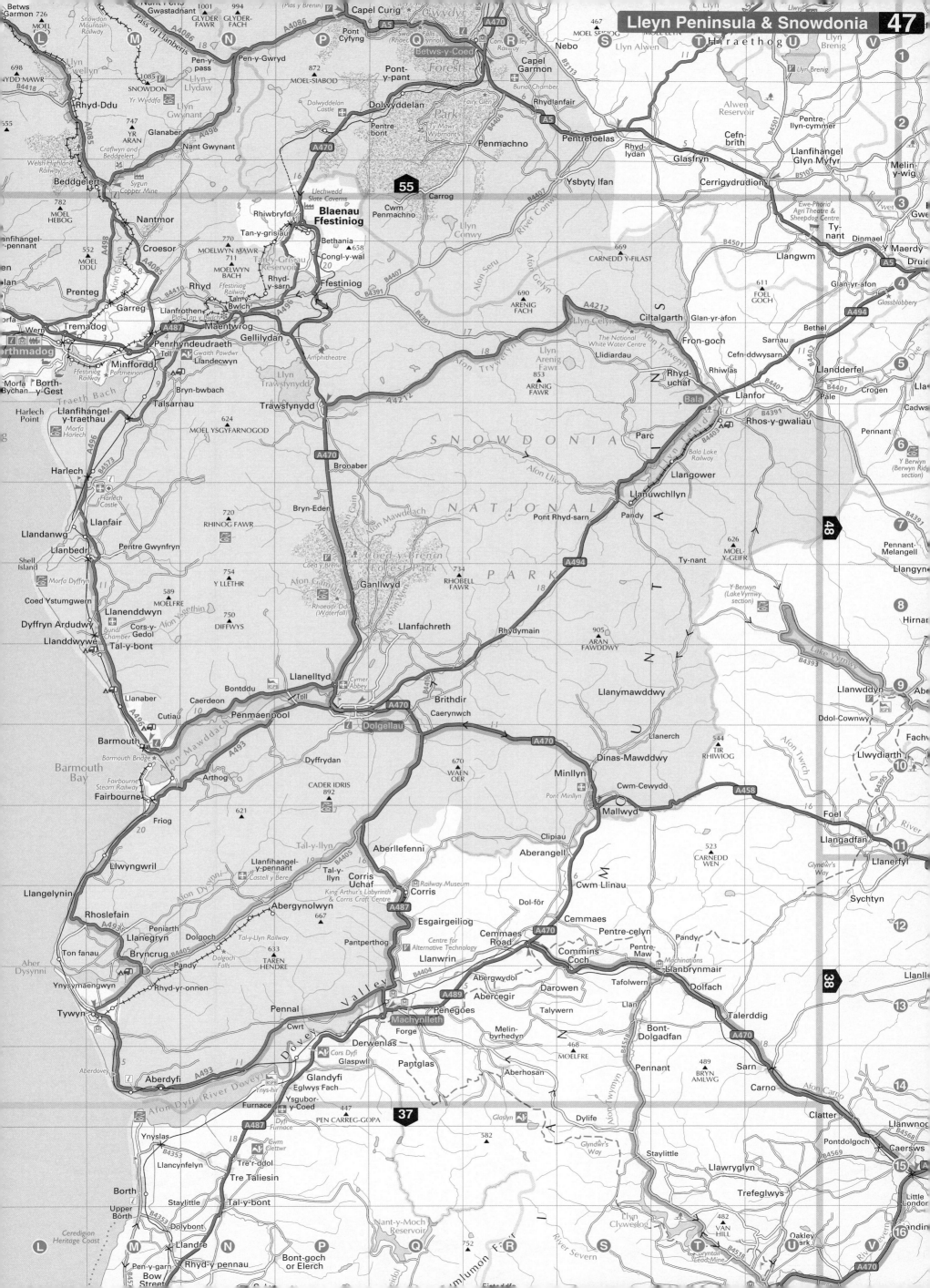

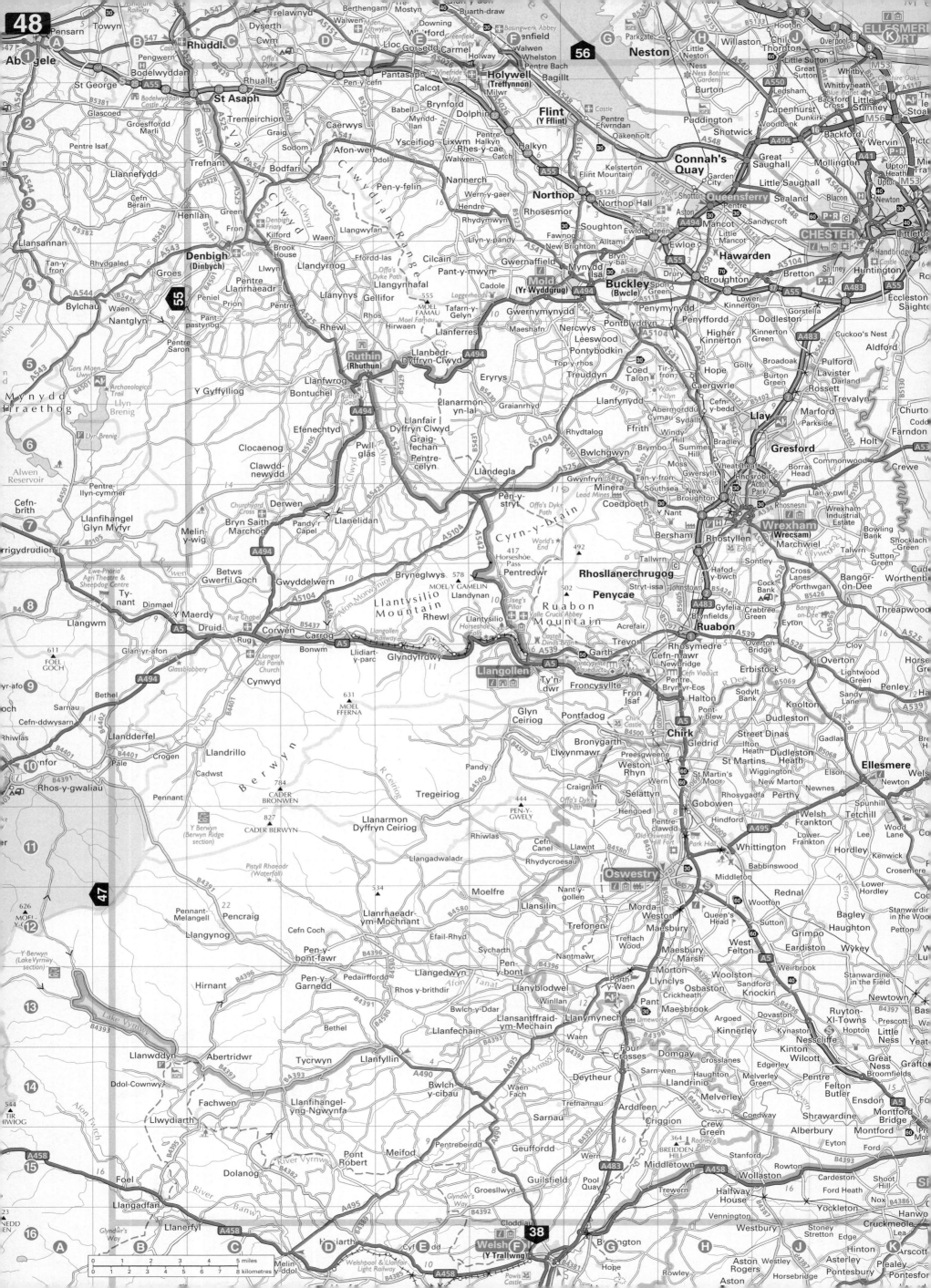

Puffin Island
Black Point
Toll
Penmon
Anglesey
Great Orme
Heritage Coast
GREAT ORMES HEAD
56
Prestatyn
Talac
A548
Gronant
Gwespyr
Llanasa
Picture
Rhyl
Gwaenysgor
Rhe
Axton
fa
gan
Meliden
Trelawnyd
Dyserth
Little Ormes Head
Penrhyn Bay
Rhôs-on-Sea
Penrhyn-side
Llandudno
Conwy Bay
Deganwy
Llanrhos
Pydew
Llandrillo-
yn-Rhos
Colwyn Bay
(Bae Colwyn)
Kinmel Bay
Abergele Roads
Towyn
Pensarn
A547
Rhuddlan
Offa's Dyke
Pengwern
A548
Berthen
Walwen
Esgyryn
Mochdre
Old Colwyn
Llandulas
Bodelwyddan
St George
Bodelwyddan Castle
St Asaph
Rhuallt
Tremeirchion
Cwm
Graig
Caerwys
Sodom
Tywyn
Llandudno
Junction
Conwy
Conwy Castle
Llansanffraid
Glan Conwy
Llanelian-
yn-Rhos
Bryn-
y-Maen
Llysfaen
Rhyd-
y-foel
Abergele
Glascoed
Groesffordd
Marli
Graig
Penmaenmawr
Dwygyfylchi
Penmaenan
Capelulo
Henryd
Dolwen
Betws-
yn-Rhos
Llanfair
Talhaiarn
Pentre Isaf
Trefnant
Bodfari
Llanfairfechan
Garizim
Nant-y-pandy
SNOWDONIA
Rowen
Ty'n-y-Groes
Dawn
Trofarth
Llannefydd
Henllan
Green
Denbigh
Friary
Kilford
Waen
Abergwyngregyn
Gorddinog
TAL-Y-FAN
Caerhun
Castell
Vale of Conwy
Pentre'r
Felin
Hafodunos
Llangernyw
Cefn
Berain
Fron
Denbigh
(Dinbych)
Castle
Brook
House
Llandyrnog
Coedydd
Aber
Aber Falls
NATIONAL
Llanbedr-y-Cennin
Tal-y-Bont
Maenan
Llansannan
Tan-y-
fron
Rhydgaled
Groes
Llwyn
Pentre
Llanrhaeadr
Peniel
Prion
Llanynys
Rachub
Y DROSGL
FOEL-FRAS
Dolgarrog
Pont Dolgarrog
River Elwy
B5382
Bylchau
Waen
Nantglyn
Pant
pastynog
Bethesda
Gerlan
Ogwen Bank
Llyn
Eigiau
PARK
Trefriw Woollen Mills
Trefriw
Llanddoget
Pandy
Tudur
B5384
Gwytherin
Pentre
Saron
Rhewl
Carnedd
Llewelyn
Afon Ddu
Llanrhychwyn
Llanrwst
Pentre-
tafarn-y-fedw
Melin-
y-coet
A543
Gors Maen
Llwyd
Archaeological
Trail
Y Gyffylliog
Ruth
(Rhuthu)
Carnedd
Dafydd
Llyn
Cowlyd
Gwydyr
Uchaf Chapel
Aon Derwyn
Aon Aled
Aon Aled
Llyn
Brenig
Llanfwrog
Bontuchel
Pont Pen-
y-benglog
Y-GARN
Y TRYFAN
National
Mountain Centre
(Plas y Brenin)
The Ugly House
(Ty Hyll)
Moel
Seisiog
Moel Llyn
Mynydd
Hiraethog
48
Efenechtyd
Pwll
glâs
Peris
astadnant
GLYDER-
FAWR
GLYDER-
FACH
Capel Curig
A5
Gwydyr
Nebo
Llyn Alwen
A543
Y Llyn
Brenig
Clocaenog
Clawdd-
newydd
A4086
Pen-y-
pass
Pen-y-Gwryd
Pont
Cyfyng
Swallow Falls
(Rhaeadr Ewynnol)
Betws-y-Coed
Forest
Capel
Garmon
Alwen
Reservoir
Pentre-
llyn-cymmer
Derwen
Llyn
Llydaw
MOEL-SIABOD
Dolwyddelan Castle
Pont-
y-pant
Burial Chamber
Fairy Glen
Rhydlanfair
Cefn-
brith
Llanfihangel
Glyn Myfyr
Melin-
y-wig
Bryn Saith
Marchog
Church
yard
Cross
Llanelidan
Llyn
Gwynant
Dolwyddelan
Pentre-
bont
Tir Mawr
Wybrnant
Penmachno
Pentrefoelas
Rhyd-
lydan
Glasfryn
Cerrigydrudion
Ewe-Phoria
Agri Theatre &
Sheepdog Centre
Ty-
nant
Pandy'r
Capel
Nant Gwynant
A470
Ysbyty Ifan
Dinmael
Y Maerdy
Betws
Gwerfil Goch
Gwyddelwern
Llechwedd
Slate Caverns
Rhiwbryfdir
Tan-y-grisiau
Carrog
Cwm
Penmachno
47
River Conwy
Llyn
Conwy
Llangwm
A5
Druid
Rug Chapel
Corwen
Carrog
Blaenau
Ffestiniog
Bethania
Congl-y-wal
MOELWYN MAWR
MOELWYN BACH
Ffestiniog
Railway
Tany-Grisiau Reservoir
Rhyd-
y-sarn
Ffestiniog
ARENIG
FACH
CARNEDD Y-FILAST
FOEL
GOCH
Glan-yr-afon
Llangar
Old Parish
Church
Bonwm
Lliaart
y-pand
Cynwyd
Llanfrothen
Plas-Tan y Bwlch
Maentwrog
Gellilydan
Afon Serw
Afon Gelyn
Llyn Celyn
The National
White Water Centre
Ciltalgarth
Glan-yr-afon
Fron-goch
Bethel
Sarnau
Cefn-d
Rhiwlas
A494
Llanderfel
Llandrillo
Penrhyndeudraeth
Llandecwyn
Amphitheatre
Afon Tryweryn
Llyn
Arenig
Fawr
ARENIG
FAWR
Llidiardau
Rhyd-
uchaf
Bala
Llanfor
Pale
Bryn-bwlch

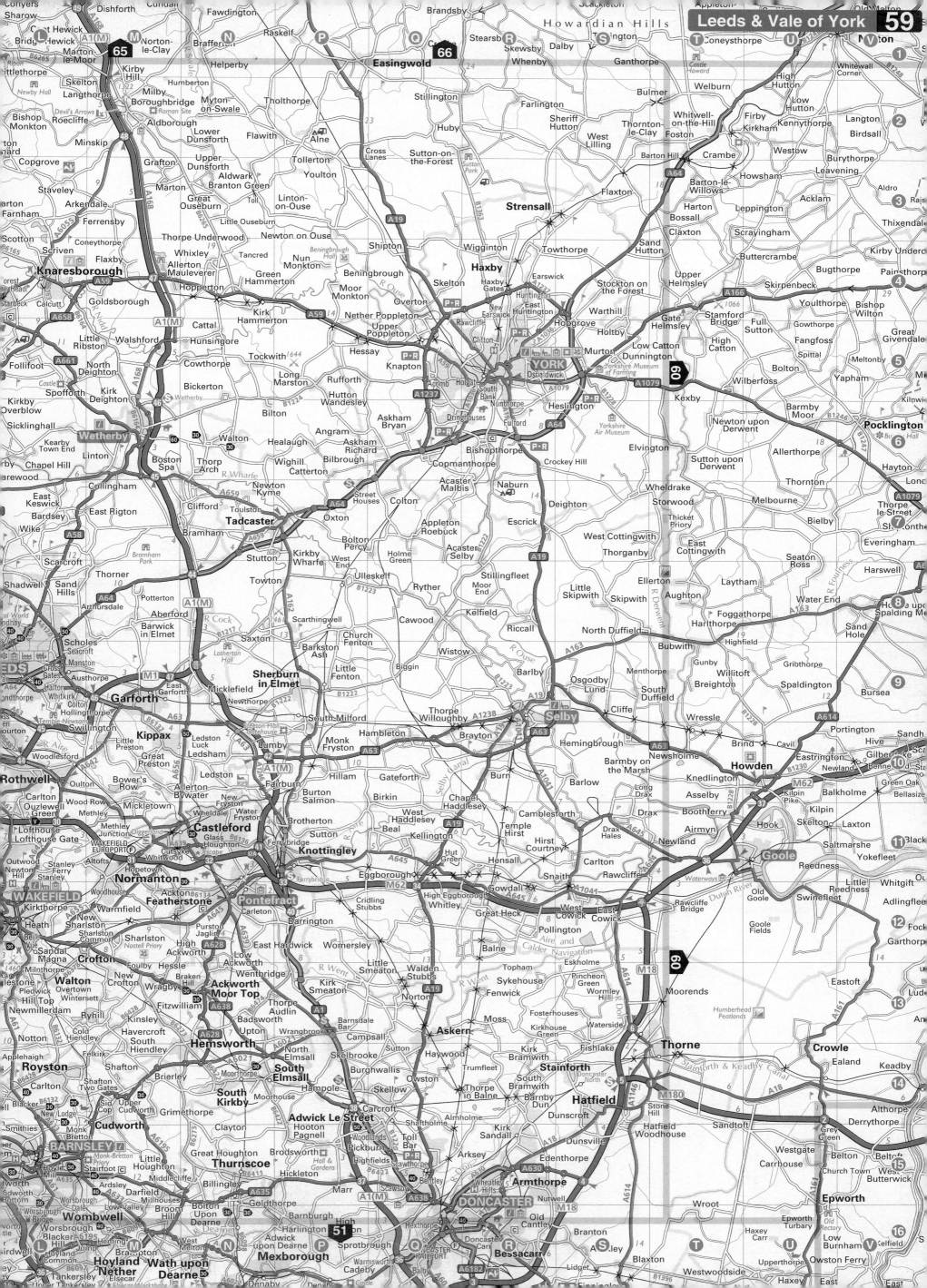

L M N P Q R S T U V

① ② ③ ④ ⑤ ⑥ ⑦ ⑧ ⑨ ⑩ ⑪ ⑫ ⑬ ⑭ ⑮ ⑯

Burton Fleming
Buckton
Bempton
North Landing
Grindale
Marton
B1229
Selwicks Bay
FLAMBOROUGH HEAD
Lighthouse
67
Sewerby
Flamborough
Boynton
Bondville Miniature Village
Bridlington
BRIDLINGTON BAY
Rudston
Monolith
Bessingby
Carnaby
Hilderthorpe
Haisthorpe
Thornholme
Norman Manor House
A165
Burton Agnes
Fraisthorpe
ham
thorpe
Little Kelk
Great Kelk
Lissett
Barmston
Gransmoor
nsford
Gembling
Ulrome
B1242
Foston on the Wolds
Skipsea
Beeford
Castle
Skipsea Brough
Upton
North Frodingham
Dunnington
Atwick
holme
Nunkeeling
Bewholme
B1242
Burshill
Honeysuckle Farm
Hornsea Mere
Hornsea
Brandesburton
Seaton
Leven
B1244
Sigglesthorne
Goxhill
Rolston
Catwick
Little Catwick
Little Hatfield
Mappleton
Mappleton Sands
Routh
Long Riston
Rise
Great Hatfield
Great Cowden
1035
Arnold
B1243
North End
H
Meaux
New Ellerby
Withernwick
Skirlaugh
O
Marton
Mount Pleasant
Wawne
L
West Newton
Aldbrough
A165
Old Ellerby
East Newton
17
hearne
Dunswell
D
Burton Constable Hall
Flinton
B1238
Garton
Swine
13
E
Thirtleby
B1242
Grimston
Coniston
Ganstead
Sproatley
Humbleton
Fitling
Hilston
40
A1033
Bransholme
Wyton
Bilton
B1240
Lelley
Owstwick
Tunstall
B1237
Sutton-on-Hull
B1238
R
Elstronwick
Danthorpe
North End
Newland
30
Stoneferry
A165
East End
Preston
Burton Pidsea
Roos
Waxholme
P·R
30
H
Marfleet
West End
Rimswell
B1242
International Ferry Terminal
A1033
Hedon
Haven Side
Burstwick
West End
Owthorne
B1362
Withernsea
KINGSTON UPON HULL
Paull
Fort Paull
Thorngumbald
Halsham
East End
B1362
Hollym
A1033
Keyingham
Ryehill
Winestead
4
New Holland
16
Ottringham
Patrington
Holmpton
North End
Goxhill
Patrington Haven
Out Newton
B1206
South End
East Halton
Sunk Island
Welwick
RIVER HUMBER
Thornton Abbey & Gatehouse
Weeton
Skeffling
Easington
B1445
Thornton Curtis
North Killingholme
Immingham Dock
South End
Spurn Heritage Coast
Ulceby Skitter
A160
Kilnsea
Ulceby
South Killingholme
Habrough
A1173
Spurn Heritage Coast
A180
SPURN HEAD
Croxton
B1211
Kirmington
B1210
Stallingborough
A180
Brocklesby
B1210
GRIMSBY
Rotterdam (Europoort) Zeebrugge
53
Keelby
Healing
West Marsh
Cleethorpes
Great Limber
52
Great Coates
Little Coates
Old Clee
Riby
Aylesby
Nunsthorpe
A46
Thrunscoe
The Jungle Pleasure Island
Humberside
A1173
A18
50
Bradley
A16
Scartho
A1098
Humberston
Laceby
B1203
New Waltham
Clixby
Irby upon Humber
Waltham
Waltham Windmill
Holton le Clay
A1031
sby
Swallow
Barnoldby le Beck
Brigsley
North
Cabourne
A18
Beelsby
Ashby cum Fenby
Tetney
Tetney Lock
Nettleton
Cuxwold
Hatcliffe
Waithe
North Cotes
Marshchapel
B1205
West Ravendale
Grainsby
North
Donna

L M N P Q R S T U V

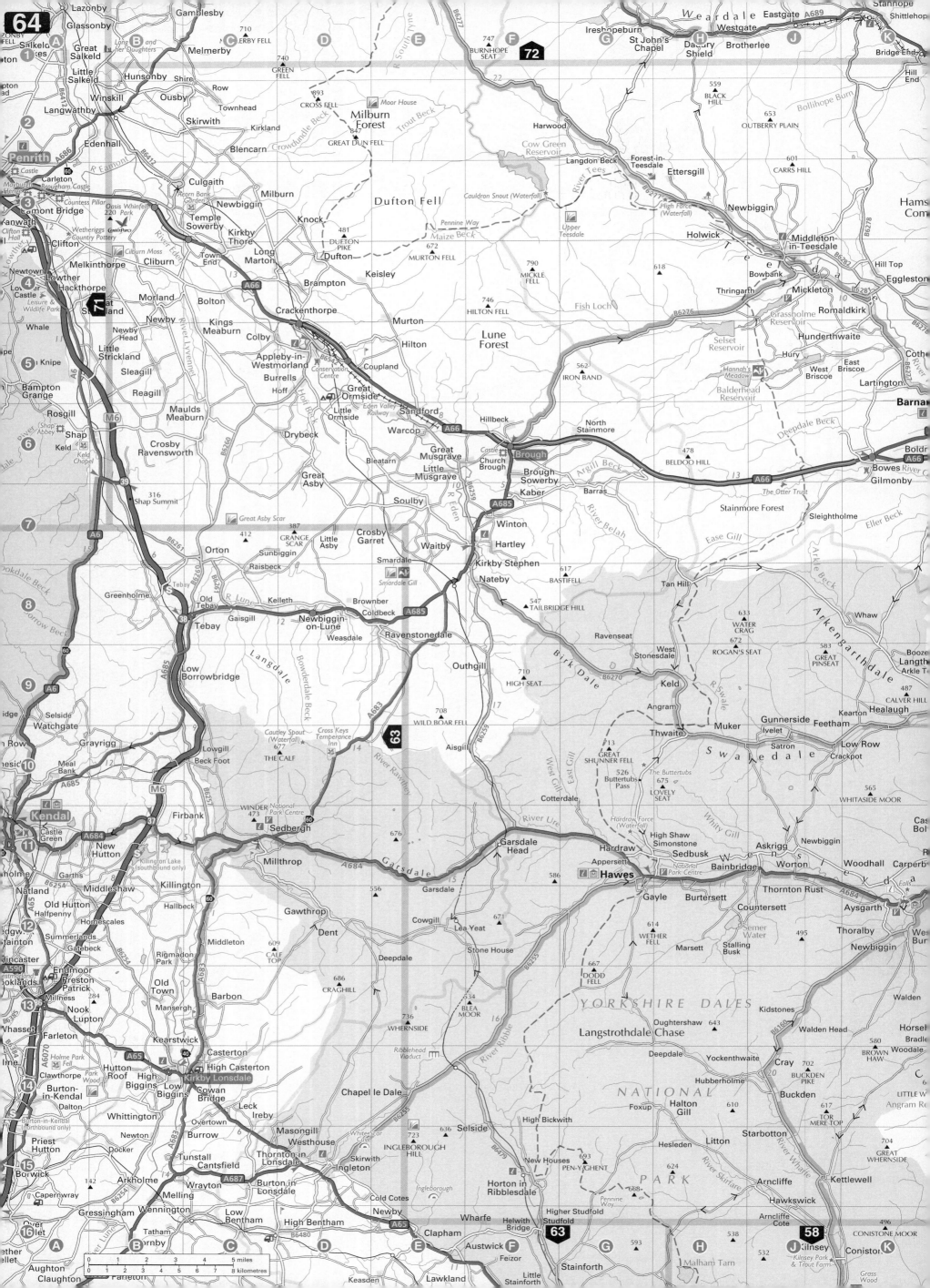

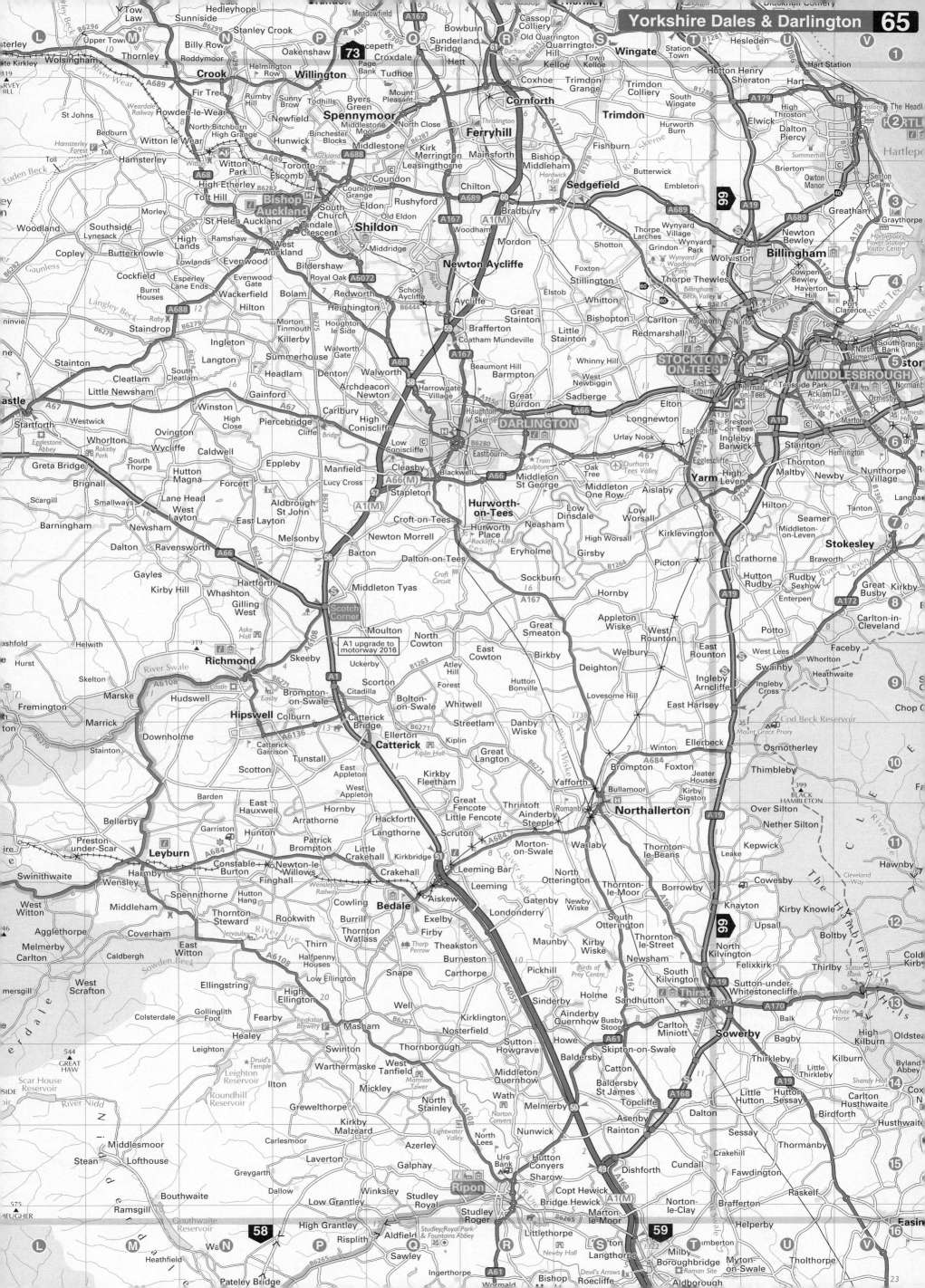

L M N P Q R S T U V

① ② ③ ④ ⑤ ⑥ ⑦ ⑧ ⑨ ⑩ ⑪ ⑫ ⑬ ⑭ ⑮ ⑯

North Yorkshire and Cleveland Heritage Coast

Goldsborough
Overdale Wyke
Lythe
Sandsend Sandsend Wyke
Raithwaite
Dunsley
Newholm
Whitby
Saltwick Bay
Abbey
Ruswarp
Briggswath Stainsacre
Aislaby
Sneaton High Hawsker
Sleights Ugglebarnby
Iburndale Low Hawsker
osmont Sneatonthorpe
Littlebeck Raw
Fylingthorpe
Ness Point or North Cheek
Robin Hood's Bay
Robin Hood's Bay
Old Peak or South Cheek
A171
Ravenscar
292
Staintondale
Shire Horse Centre
Hayburn Wyke
Harwood Dale Cloughton Newlands
Bridestones (Rock Formation)
Bickley
Broxa Silpho
Hackness Suffield
Langdale End
Wrench Green
Everley
Cloughton
Cloughton Wyke
Cromer Point
Burniston
A165
Cleveland Way
Newby
Scalby
Castle
Scarborough
Falsgrave
Hatherleigh Deep Sea Trawler
North Riding Forest Park
239
Oliver's Mount
Dalby Forest Drive
Toll
Dalby Forest
Bee Dale
A170
West Ayton
P·R
East Ayton
Eastfield
A165
Osgodby
Cayton Bay
Irton
Sawdon
Hutton Buscel
Seamer
Crossgates
Cayton
The Wyke
Wilton
Ebberston Ruston
Snainton Wykeham
Brompton-by-Sawdon
High Killerby
Filey Brigg
Allerston B1415
A1039
Lebberston
Gristhorpe
Filey
Yedingham
Folkton
Muston
Willerby
A1039
West Flotmanby
Filey Bay
Flixton
Staxton
West Knapton Knapton
Sherburn
Ganton
Yorkshire Wolds Way
Hunmanby
East Heslerton
Potter Brompton
Fordon
Reighton
West Heslerton
Flamborough Head Heritage Coast
Thorpe Bassett Wintringham
Foxholes
Wold Newton
Speeton
Bempton Cliffs
Thornwick Bay
Scagglethorpe Newton
Butterwick
Burton Fleming
Buckton
Bempton
North Landing
Settrington
Helperthorpe
Weaverthorpe
Thwing
Grindale
A165
Selwicks Bay
60
West Lutton East Lutton
Octon
Marton
FLAMBOROUGH HEAD
North Grimst
Duggleby
Kirby Grindalythe
Langtoft
B1253
Rudston
Monolith
Boynton
Bondy Miniature Village
Flamborough
Wharram
Bessingby
61
Bridlington
BRIDLINGTON

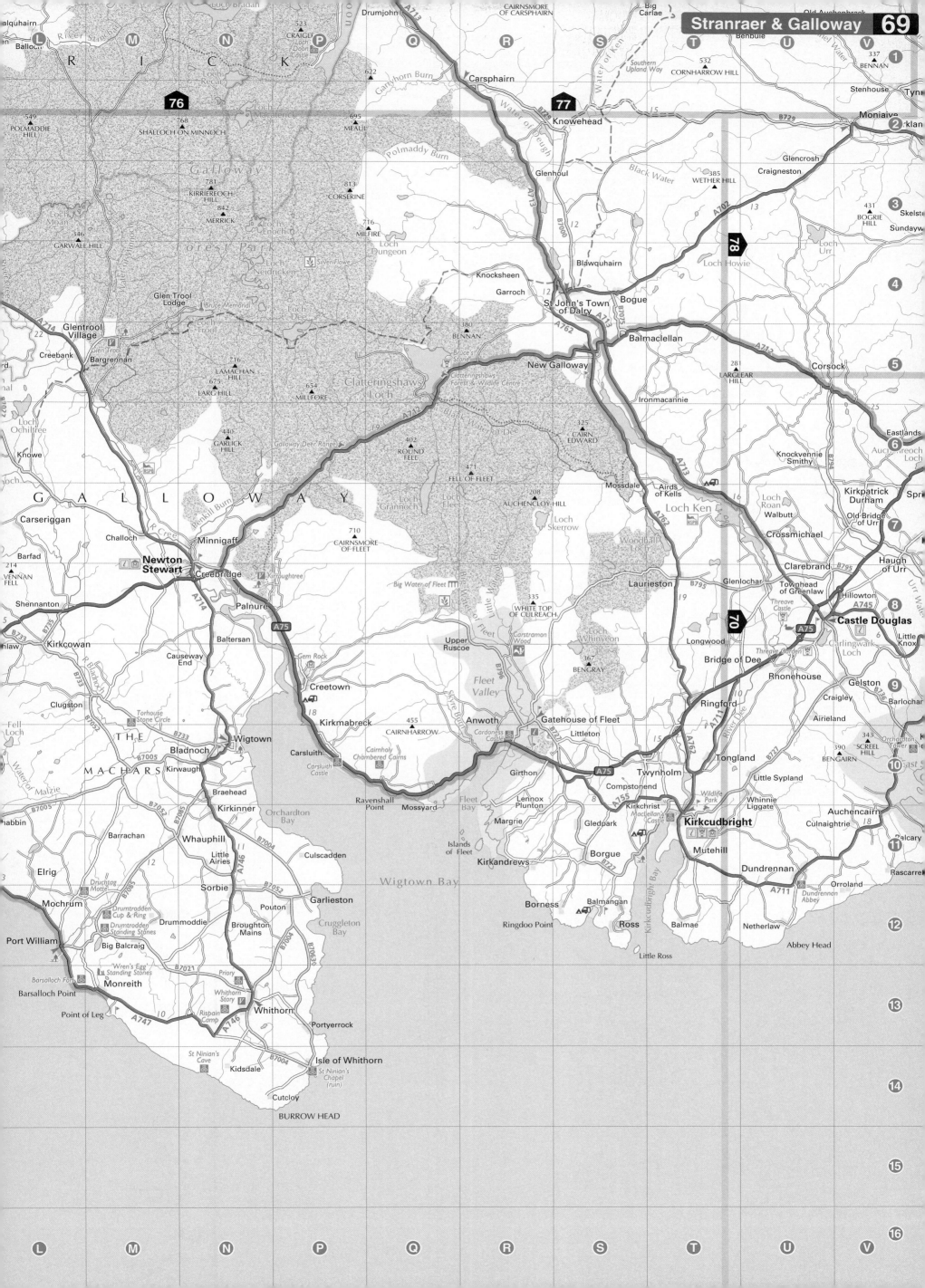

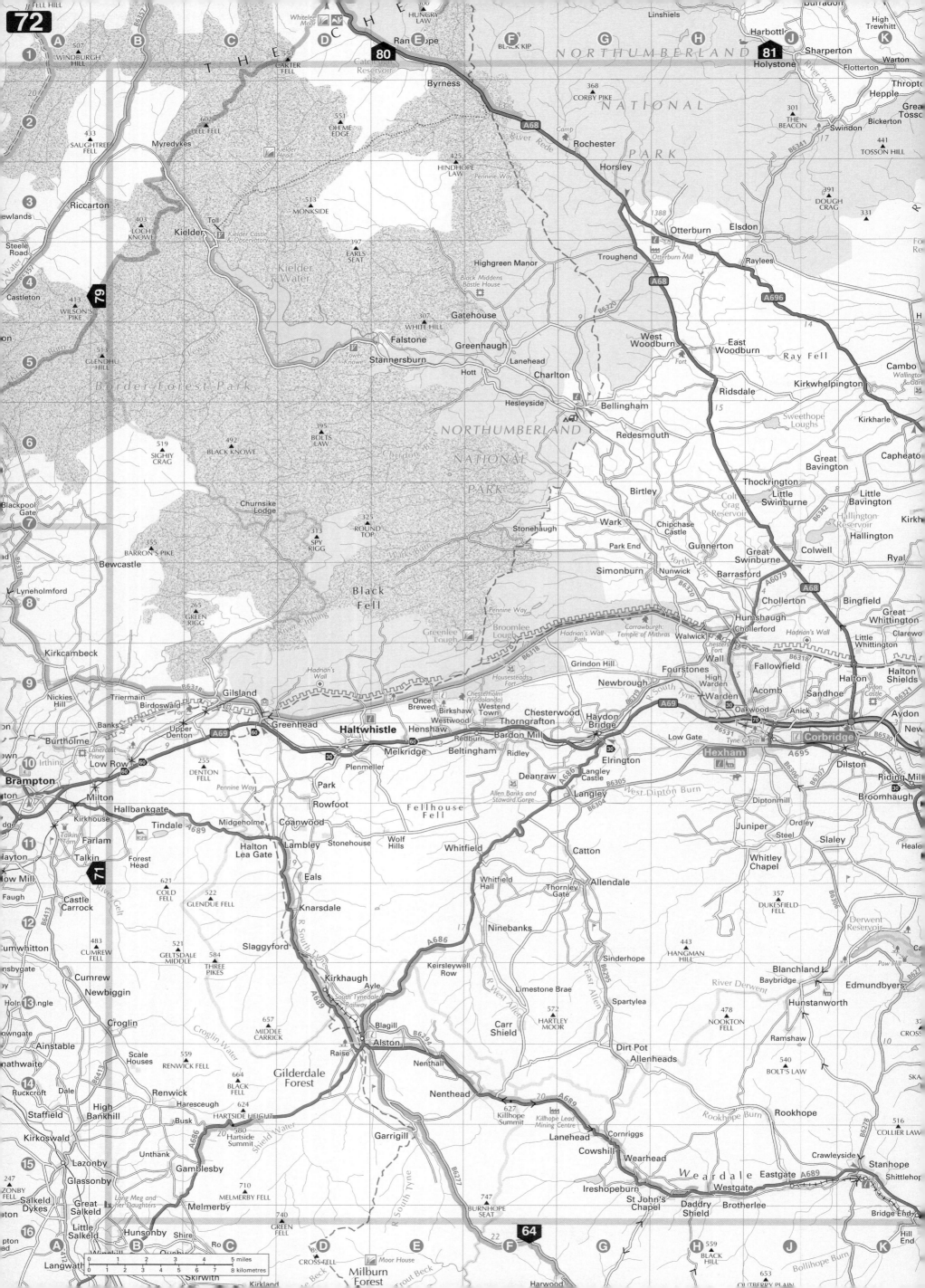

Rothesay

Ardlamont Point

Ullanlay
Meikle Kilmory
Midpark
Loch Fad
Inchmarnock
Kingart
Kilchattan
Ardscalpsie Bay
Stravanan Bay
St Blane's Church
Garrochty
Garroch Head

83

84

Sound of Bute

Kilberry
Torinturk
Kilberry Head
213
Keppoch Point
CRUACH AIRDE
Tiretigan
Whitehouse
nacraig
422
CNOC A' BHAILE-SHOIS
Kilchamaig
Ardpatrick
Skipness
Castle
Chapel
Skipness Point
Portachoillan
Clachan
Claonaig
B8001
Ronachan Point
Ronachan
B842
Cock of Arran
Lochranza
Castle
Catacol
Loch Ciaran
Loch Garasdale
Glen Chalmadale 8
Crossaig
Glen Catacol
Sannox
A841
247
CRUACH MHIC GOUGAIN
264
CNOC-AN T-SAMHLAIDH
Cour Bay
Cour
Pirnmill
Penrioch
North Arran
834
CAISTEAL ABHAIL
Loch Tanna
Corrie
Grogport
Barmollack
715
BEINN BHARRAIN
Glen Iorsa
874
GOATFELL
Whitefarland
792
BEINN NUIS
Glen Rosa
Merkland Point
354
CRUACH NAN GABHAR
Imachar
Balliekine
6
Brodick Castle, Garden & Country Club
Brodick Bay
Muasdale
Carradale
Carradale Water
B879
Carradale House
Iorsa Water
A R R A N
Strathwhillan
Glenacardoch Point
Belloch
Barr Water
Bridgend
Dippen
Carradale Point
Machrie Bay
Auchogallon Stone Circle
Machrie
Brodick
Corriegills
76
Glenbarr
MacAlister Clan
454
BEINN AN TUIRC
Torrisdale
Carradale Bay
Machrie Moor Stone Circles
Tormore
11
512 A'CHRUACH
Clauchlands Point
319
408 BORD MOR
Saddell
Moss Farm Road Stone Circle
Balmichael
503 BEINN BHREAC
Margnaheglish
Lamlash
Bellochantuy
Saddell Bay
Torbeg
Balmichael
Lamlash Bay
Holy Island
Bellochantuy Bay
Shiskine
Cordon
396 SGREADAN HILL
Ugadale
Blackwaterfoot
4
Kilpatrick
Auchencairn
Kingscross
Kilkenzie
Glen Lussa
Peninver
Drumadoon Bay
Kilpatrick Dun
Carn Ban
Knockenkelly
Ardnacross Bay
Glen Scorrodale
Whiting Bay
Glen Ashdale
A83
Kilmichael
Brown Head
Largymore
Machrihanish Bay
Campbeltown
Corriecravie
Kilmory Water
Largybeg
Machrihanish
Campbeltown Loch
Sliddery
Dippen
Dippen Head
Drumlemble
B843
Kilkerran
Island Davarr
Torr a' Chaisteal Fort
Lagg
Torrylin Cairn
Kilmory
Bennan
Kildonan
B842
Kildalloig
352 BEINN GHUILEAN
Bennan Head
Pladda
385 THE STATE
Achinhoan
446 CNOC MOY
Ru Stafnish
Dalsmeran
Glen Kerran
Conie Glen
Glen Breakerie
Cattadale
Polliwilline Bay
Strone Glen
NA LICE
Carskey
Dunaverty
Southend
Macharioch
Carskey Bay
Sanda Sound
Sheep Island
Borgadalemore Point
Sanda Island

340 Ailsa Craig
RSPB

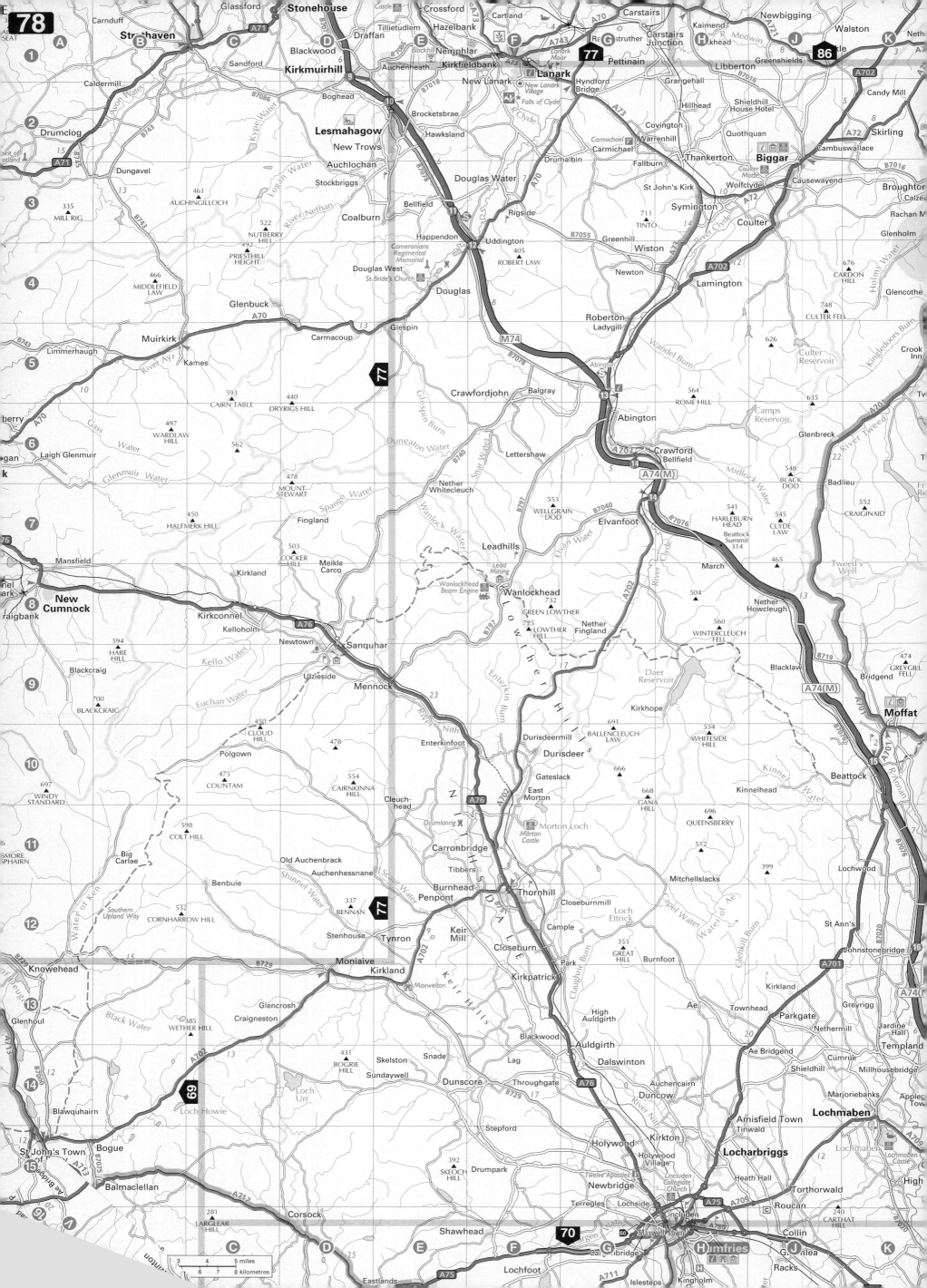

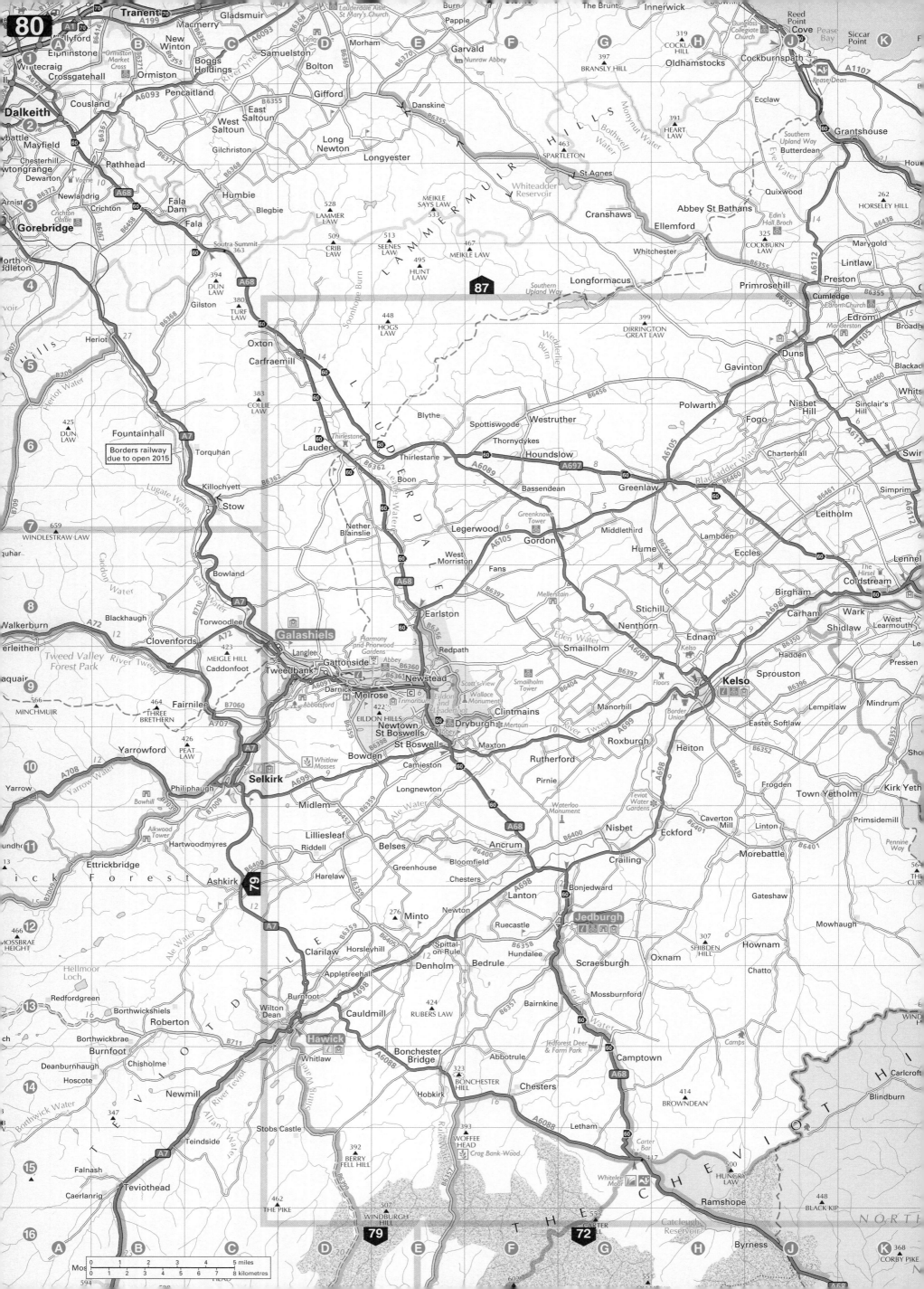

L M N P Q R S T U V
1
2
3
4
5
6
7
8
9
10
11
12
13
14
15
16

93

Kingsharns
Balcomie
Links
FIFE NESS
Crail
Dunir.
Kingsmuir
Scotland's
Secret Bunker
Carnbee
Easter Pitkierie
Kellie
Castle
Wester
Pitkierie
Kilrenny
Cellardyke
Newton of
Balcormo
Fisheries
Anstruther
Pittenweem
St Monans
Elie
Earlsferry

Peat
Inn
Radernie
Lathones
Largoward
Lochty
Arncroach
Colinsburgh
Drumeldrie
Kilconquhar
Bay

Isle of May

Fidra
Craigleith
Bass Rock
Eyebroughy
North Berwick
Dirleton Castle
& Gardens
Scottish-Seabird
Tantallon Castle
Gullane Bay
Dirleton
Muirfield
NORTH
BERWICK
LAW
Cleghornie
Gullane Point
Gullane
Fenton
Barns
Kingston
Whitekirk
Aberlady Bay
Luffness
Drem
Prora
East
Fortune
St Baldred's Cradle
Tyne Mouth
Belhaven
Bay
Point
Aberlady
Spittal
Ballencrieff
Chesters
Hill Fort
Preston Mill
& Phantassie
Doocot
Museum
of Flight
Markle
Tyninghame
John Muir
Belhaven
Dunbar
Longniddry
Huntington
Elvingston
Athelstaneford
East Linton
West Barns
Broxburn
Barns Ness
Macmerry
Haddington
St Martin's Kirk (ruin)
Traprain
A199
Hailes
Castle
Pitcox
Spott
Doonhill
Homestead
A1
East Barns
Skateraw
Chapel Point
New
inton
Gladsmuir
Lauderdale Aisle
St Mary's Church
Traprain
Law
Luggate
Burn
Stenton
The Brunt
Innerwick
Dry Burn
Thorntonloch
Crowhill
Cove
Reed
Point
Pease
Bay
Siccar
Point
Fast Castle Head
Boggs
Holdings
Samuelston
Morham
Papple
Garvald
Nunraw Abbey
319
COCKLAW
HILL
Oldhamstocks
Dunglass
Collegiate
Church
Cockburnspath
A1107
Pease
Dean
196 Coldingham
BROWN Loch
RIG
ST ABBS HEAD
Bolton
397
BRANSLY HILL
Pencaitland
Gifford
391
HEART
LAW
Ecclaw
Grantshouse
St ABBS HEAD
St Abbs
Coldingham
Bay
West
Saltoun
East
Saltoun
463
SPARTLETON
Bothwell
Water
Monynut Water
Southern
Upland Way
Eye Water
Butterdean
Houndwood
Coldingham
Gilchriston
Long
Newton
Danskine
St Agnes
Quixwood
Heugh
Head
Cairncross
Humbie
Whiteadder
Reservoir
391
Cranshaws
Abbey St Bathans
325
COCKBURN
LAW
Horseley Hill
Reston
Ayton
Fala
Dam
Blegbie
528
LAMMER
LAW
MEIKLE
SAYS LAW
533
Ellemford
Edin's
Hall Broch
14
Auchencrow
Fala
509
CRIB
LAW
513
SEENES LAW
467
MEIKLE LAW
Whitchester
Marygold
Lintlaw
Soutra Summit
363
495
HUNT
LAW
Longformacus
Southern
Upland Way
Primrosehill
Preston
Chirnside
394
DUN
LAW
A68
448
HOGS
LAW
399
DIRRINGTON
GREAT LAW
80
Cumledge
Edrom
Church
Chirnsidebridge
Foulden
Gilston
380
TURF
LAW
Oxton
Wedderlie
Burn
Whiteadder
Water
Carfraemill
Broadhaugh
Edington
Allanton
Hutton
Pax
Duns
Manderston
383
COLLIE
LAW
Blythe
Westruther
Gavinton
Blackadder
Whitsome
Hilton
Horndean
Hornel
Lauder
Thirlestane
Spottiswoode
Thornydykes
Houndslow
Polwarth
Fogo
Nisbet
Hill
Sinclair's
Hill
Ladykirk
Swinton
Norham
Torquhan
Boon
A6089
A697
Bassendean
Greenlaw
Charterhall
Leitholm
Upsettlington
Killochyett
Stow
Nether
Blainslie
Legerwood
Gordon
West
Morriston
Fans
Middlethird
Hume
Lambden
Eccles
Lennel
Simprim
Grindon
Shellacres
79
Bowland
Greenknowe
Tower
Donaldson's
Lodge
The
Hirsel
Coldstream

81

CANNA
CÀRN A' GHAILL
Garrisdale Point
A'Chill
Canna Harbour
Sanday
Sound of Canna
Kilmory Bay
Rudha Shamhnan Insir

MULLACH MÒR
302
A Bhrideanach
570
ORVAL
Kinloch
Loch Scresort
Rudha na Roinne

RÙM
810
ASKIVAL

Harris Bay
763
SGÙRR NAN GILLEAN

The Small Isles
Rudha nam Meirleach

Sound of Rum

Bay of Laig
Rudha an Fhasaidh
Laig
EIGG

Sound of Eigg
393
AN SGÙRR

Eilean nan Each
MUCK
Port Mor

Oigh-sgeir

Sanna Point
Sanna Bay
Sanna Bay
Portuairk
Achna
Ardnamurchan Point
Achosnich

Bagh a Chaisteil (Castlebay)
Loch Baghasdail (Lochboisdale)

Eilean Mòr
342
BEINN NA-SEILG

Rudha Mòr
Rudha Sgor-innis
Bousd
Sorisdale

Cliad Bay
Arnabost
Ardmore Point

Grishipoll
Sorne Point
Glengorm Castle

Clabhach
Loch Cliad
Quinish Point

Iogh Bay
Ballyhaugh
Arinagour
COLL
Coll–Oban
292
'S AIRD BEINN

Totronald
Caliach Point

Arileod
Coll
Acha
Eilean Ornsay
Caliach Point
Dervaig
Achnadris

Uig
5

Bagh a Chaisteil (Castlebay)
Calgary
Calgary

Calgary Point
Crossapoll Bay
Rudha Fàsachd
Calgary Bay

Gunna
Loch Beag na Cha
Rudha Dubh
Treshnish Point
Ensay
342
CÀRN MÒR

Rudha Port Bhiosd
Clachan Mòr
Caoles
Rudh' a' Chaoil
Burg

Loch Bhasapoll
Balephetrish Bay
B8069
Ruaig
Fanmore
390
CNOC AN DÀ CHINN

Haugh Bay
Ballevullin
Cornoigmore
Kenovay
Gott Bay
Fladda
Ballygown
Eas Fors (Waterfa

Kilkenneth
Tiree
Lunga
Loch Tuath

Moss
Heylipoll
Scarinish
TRESHNISH ISLES
Gometra
ULVA
Oskamull

Middleton
Crossapoll
Hynish Bay

Barrapoll
TIREE

Loch a' Phuill
Balemartine
Bac Mòr or Dutchmans Cap

Rinn Thorbhais
Mannel
Bac Beag

Balephuil Bay
Hynish
Little Colonsay
Inch Kenneth
Inchkenneth Chapel (ruin)

Staffa
Loch na Keal, Isle of Mull
Balnahard

Fingal's Cave

519
BEIN NA SREINE

491
CREACH BHEINN
Fossil Tree
Burg

Rudha nan Cearc
IONA
Iona Abbey & Nunnery
Kintra
Loch Scri

Baile Mòr
MacLean's Cross
Fionnphort
Ardglas
376
CRUACHAN MIN

St Columba Exhibition Centre
Bunessan
Loch Assapol

Soa Island
ROSS OF MULL
Uisken

Erraid
Ardchiavaig
Rudha nam Braithrean

Rudha Ardalanish

Torran Rocks

0 1 2 3 4   5 miles
0 1 2 3 4 5 6 7 8 kilometres